The
WRINKLIES'™
GUIDE TO

Home Computing

New pursuits for old hands

Guy Croton

PRION

First published in Great Britain in 2012

Prion Books
an imprint of the
Carlton Publishing Group
20 Mortimer Street
London W1T 3JW

A catalogue record of this book is available from the British Library.

ISBN: 978 1 85375 836 2

Printed in the UK by CPI Group (UK) Ltd, Croydon, CR0 4YY

10 9 8 7 6 5 4 3 2 1

CONTENTS

FOREWORD

My adult life has been transformed by the home computer. Yours can be too. I say adult life because I wasn't an enthusiast for the personal computer of sorts we had at school. About the size of a fridge/freezer, it had spinning wheels of punched paper tape on the front, and was assigned a room of its own. It was strictly the preserve of the school's nerdiest pupils whose lack of personal hygiene was noxiously exaggerated by its prodigious heat output. I found it could do nothing useful for me, and left it well alone.

For me it all started with word processing. When I was a TV director in the 1980s tweaking a script meant hours of tedious retyping with my portable typewriter. Home computers were just becoming affordable and the discovery that I could use my newly acquired toy for basic word processing as well as gaming was sheer delight. Now, with just a few keystrokes, I could change my scripts completely. If that was all that home computers had achieved they would have transformed my life.

But then came email and the internet. I signed up at home in the mid-1990s when people were already sharing vast amounts of material online. At last my thirst for information could be satisfied. Questions which had once prompted a trip to the library or the purchase of expensive books could now be answered in seconds, usually for free.

Soon, home computers were becoming more powerful and internet connections faster. High-resolution photos could now be sent, received and processed at home. This was another revelation. It meant I could rediscover the joys of photography, an enthusiasm I'd let lapse on leaving college when I no longer had access to a traditional darkroom. Now I could manipulate my digital images with far greater precision on my laptop, and all without contaminating the spare bedroom with venomous developing fluids.

Home computers have become better at tackling a burgeoning variety of tasks: shopping for a wider range of products at cheaper prices, watching movies on demand, making free video calls to family the other side of the world, tracing lost friends, editing home movies, keeping up with the news, banking and trading... The list is endless.

Now, I know some people think computers are rather daunting. But I strongly believe that this isn't the case today. As they've become more capable and powerful computers have also become much easier to use.

Guy Croton does a splendid job of leading you gently on one of the most satisfying voyages of discovery you'll ever take. Soon, you'll find that you're mastering your computer better than some younger members of the family and that you can enjoy your advisory role as a digital *éminence grise*.

So, go for it. Don't miss out. Believe me, the rewards are amazing.

Jon Bentley

INTRODUCTION

Do you remember *2001: A Space Odyssey*, Stanley
Kubrick's 1968 cinematic masterpiece, set in outer space?
It featured a computer named the HAL 9000, or "Hal"
for short, which was in control of a spaceship on its
way to Jupiter with an otherwise human crew, some of
them suspended in cryogenic animation. As the journey
progresses, Hal, who has a range of responses and
"emotions" that are near-human, starts to go mad and
begins to bump off the human members of the crew, one by
one. It's powerful, emotive stuff, and the way in which Hal's
gradual descent into paranoid digital insanity is portrayed
is really quite disturbing – a computer that takes over a
spaceship and systematically murders its crew? It's enough
to put you off artificial intelligence for life ...!

What are we to do?
You have just picked up a guide to home computing with the
word "wrinklies" on the cover, so we are guessing that you
are at least of a reasonably advanced vintage. You've been
around the block a bit and you know a thing or two. But do
you know anything about computers? Maybe not, as you
have chosen to investigate this handy little tome. Perhaps the
story above has some resonance with you – maybe you are
actually a little fearful of these infernal boxes of electronic
tricks, which, just like Hal running "his" spaceship,

now seem to run the entire world. You may not quite be suspended in cryogenic animation, like some of Hal's human colleagues, but perhaps secretly you wish you were, as this modern world of technology courts you with confusion and blinds you with its high-tech, mysterious ways …

If this sounds like you, fear not – you have come to the right place! In this book we will show you everything you need to know about computers, and probably quite a bit that you don't, as well. In these pages we demystify the demons, junk the jargon and curtail the criteria. In other words, we take all the stuff and nonsense out of the world of computing and instead present you with a coherent, easy-to-follow guide to computers, carefully designed to appeal and make sense to "silver surfers", just like you.

Does exactly what it says on the tin

We begin this crusade into the world of computing with a thorough introduction to the nuts and bolts of this modern phenomenon. What sort of computer should you buy? What defines the specification of a computer? What exactly are all its functions and, most importantly of all, what do you want to use a computer for? Sound buying advice is accompanied by jargon-busting, step-by-step explanations and analysis of the real stuff that you need to know in order to become a fully-fledged member of computer world.

Once you have actually acquired your gleaming, sleek, new electronic steed, we show you in detail how and where to set it up, with comprehensive information about installing software, peripheral devices and much, much more.

Then, a series of chapters shows you exactly how to operate your new toy or tool, with full guidance on the wonders of email and the extraordinary global phenomenon that is the World Wide Web or Internet. Whether you want to shop online, bet online, meet that special someone online or simply "silver surf" to your heart's content, we show you how. We even set you some simple technical challenges and show you the best of the Internet for the older generation.

If you want to use your computer to edit photos, manipulate music or even make movies, we explain how to become the next David Bailey, Paul McCartney or Steven Spielberg – well, in principle, anyway! In a nutshell, whatever you want to do with your computer, we have got it covered in this little book – and we guarantee that we will take away the fear factor and give you the confidence that you need to operate your new machine with complete satisfaction.

Conclusion

Just because you are getting older, there is no reason why you should not embrace computers and enjoy the advantages that they bestow in so many areas of contemporary life. Indeed, if you don't learn how to use a computer – and more particularly, if you don't discover how to engage confidently with the Internet – you will actually be missing out on much of the best that this curious modern world has to offer. Yes, it's true that fewer old people use computers and the Internet; yes, it's true that many of the functions of computers have not really been designed with the older generation in mind; yes, it's true that some websites are garish, inaccessible and unappealing to the older viewer. However, these are all shibboleths of technology that can so easily be overcome if only you know the right places to look and the right ways to go about things in cyberspace. *The Wrinklies' Guide to Home Computing* takes care of all that and shows you everything you need to know. Simply read on ...

Happy computing!

Chapter 1

CHOOSING AND BUYING A COMPUTER

The modern world is frankly a pretty confusing place for many of us, no part more so than that ever-growing and ubiquitous area which is devoted to computers and that mysterious otherworld known as the Internet. For someone who grew up at a time when the fountain pen was really the only communication tool you needed and a monogram record player was about the most advanced household appliance you could buy, computers and their endless progeny can represent a significant challenge.

The other aspect of computerization and general Internetry that leaves us scratching our heads is the speed with which it has all happened! How did we come to such a pass so quickly? One minute you were sitting at home happily clattering away on your old Remington typewriter, while idly watching black-and-white television or changing 45rpm vinyl discs on your turntable, the next you're faced with a multicoloured, flashing and beeping computer screen, taking you to corners of the world that you never even knew existed, while playing you music and showing you films on something called "YouTube" that are conjured up by simply tapping their names into a keyboard. The phrase "Pandora's Box" springs to mind – or maybe even Ali Baba's magic cavern!

You will probably have heard of the Second World War German Enigma code machine, and the magnificent efforts of the early computer scientist Alan Turing and his team at Bletchley Park, whose decoding of many secret messages significantly affected the course of the war. Well, this is really where computers all started, and in the context of this little book that is probably all you need to know about their early history. Suffice to say that very little seemed to happen in the world of computers between the 1940s and the 1980s – at least in the public consciousness – but in the last 25 years or so there has been a massive explosion in this area of technology, and most particularly in global communications.

So, do you want to become part of this amazing new world? Are you ready to slough off certain ways of living that served you so well for so many decades and replace them with a whole new manner of doing things? If the answer to these questions is "yes", it's time to buy a computer!

What Do You Want to Do?

Before you go out and start splashing your hard-earned cash on some sleek, shining beast of a machine, you need to have a good, hard think about what you want to use a computer for. The abilities of most modern computers are about as myriad and diverse as their specifications and prices, so by narrowing down the functions that you will require, you should also gain a clearer idea about the nature of the machine you will need and the amount of money that it will cost. You see, as with everything else in the modern world, there is just so much choice in computer world that it is hard to know where to begin! However, follow the practical advice in this book and you should not go too far wrong.

With a modern computer, you can do any and all of the following:

- **Keep in contact with friends and family.** You have probably heard of something called "email", even if you have never actually used it. The "e" in question is short for "electronic", and the mail means just what it says. Put simply, this is a worldwide, Internet-based system that enables you to send messages to anyone you care to via a computer keyboard. Emails can be sent to other computers, electronic notepads, mobile phones and one or two other electronic media that we shall consider later on. In addition to messages, you can also share video images via web cams (tiny, inexpensive video cameras that capture and send your image to another computer), as well as sending photographs, video clips and electronic files as attachments to your emails. You can even "chat" in real time with others by typing messages and sending them through your computer using a technology called instant messaging. Incredible, isn't it!

- **Use the Internet like a library.** If you have trouble grasping the enormity of the concept of the Internet

– which appropriately, in terms of its degree of complexity, is also known as the "World Wide Web" – think of it as a gigantic, all-encompassing library, or series of libraries across the world, that are all linked together by an infinite network of electronic connections. In this "super-library", you can find many well-crafted and reputable websites (individual "homes" of information that we shall explore in detail later) that will give you information on absolutely anything you care to ask. When presented with an Internet browser (means of Internet access) on a computer for the first time in his life in 1990, this author tapped the word "sharks" into the keyboard, for no other reason than that he finds them fascinating and it was the first word that came into his head! Suddenly, a plethora of links to websites devoted to sharks sprang up on the screen before him, accompanied by a wealth of glossy images. With his jaw dropping in amazement, your correspondent cast about the office in which he was sitting, in search of another suitable topic to browse. Somewhat prosaically, his eye alighted on the coffee mug beside him, so he entered the word "coffee", only to be rewarded with a similarly astounding set of results. Take our word for it, whatever you want to research on the Internet – no matter how large or how minuscule – you will always find something ...

- **Create and share photos, videos and drawings.** If you have a digital camera, you can easily transfer photos to your computer via a simple process called "uploading". You can then attach these to emails and send them to your friends and family. Alternatively, you can "download" images from the Internet and share those or maybe use them to create your own greeting cards, which can also be conveyed digitally across the world to any specific electronic destination that you choose. If you are artistically inclined, you can also create digital drawings and send these. Finally, and perhaps most incredibly of all, you can even upload entire digital videos online, which you have recorded on your video camera. You can put these up on the Internet in their raw state, where they can be shared by anyone you choose to contact about them, or you can use editing tools in video software on your computer to polish up your efforts a little before uploading them. You can probably see by now that computers and the Internet enable you to become not only a universal correspondent, but also a one-stop photo agency, amateur artist and budding film director!

- **Shop online and compare products.** One of the very best things about the Internet is that it allows you to buy just about anything from the comfort of your own armchair. This can be a very handy feature indeed for a member of the older generation, particularly if you are at all immobile or have a disability of some kind. Price comparison websites – which you will doubtless have seen advertised on the television, either by irritating Russian meerkats or an even more infuriating overweight, Italian pseudo-opera singer – also make it possible to compare a multitude of prices for just about any item. This can save you a fortune. Of course, the

downside of shopping online is that you cannot see
and feel the quality of the goods, although, having
said that, most websites post a variety of images of the
products that they sell, which will facilitate your selection.
You normally have to pay postage and packing on top of
the price of the article you are purchasing, but if you have
found a bargain, this cost will normally be offset by your
savings and the expense and hassle of having to leave
your house and go to the shops instead.

- **Control your finances.** Not so many years ago, there
  were enough scare stories in the newspapers about
  "hacking", "phishing" and other intriguingly named
  computer phenomena to make us think we would
  never entrust our finances to the Internet in a million
  years. However, the security systems of both the
  Internet at large and the world's financial institutions
  have come a very long way in a very short space of
  time. Provided your computer is protected by up-to-
  date anti-virus software and firewalls (more of which
  later), you can now conduct your banking, building
  society and share dealing transactions online with
  more or less complete peace of mind. Again, rather like
  shopping, this is one of the great boons of the Internet,
  especially for the less energetic among us who might
  balk at the prospect of queueing up at the bank or
  trudging off to see the accountant.

- **Play interactive games.** If you are wearied by whist,
  bored with backgammon, chary of chess or dread
  draughts, you could always try playing some of the

multitude of interactive, electronic games that are now available on the Internet. It's a strange concept, but you might find yourself trading moves online with a shopkeeper in Kazakhstan or a farmer in New Zealand, as you get to grips with your latest interactive game choice. You can even join "virtual" communities and "second worlds" – faintly alarming simulacrums of real life in which you can play the part of an alter ego of your choice or just about any other character. Once you get online, take a look at some of the slightly less disturbing versions of these "virtual worlds", such as "Second Life" or "FarmVille". In the former of these you can embark on a whole new virtual existence – where you can be any age you choose! – or in the latter, you can actually run your own virtual farm. Incredible, but true …

- **Join online chat rooms and interactive blogs.** If you have a particular interest or passion – anything from cars to cats, with cassowaries in between – you can find online "chat rooms" and interactive "blogs", where you can meet like-minded folk who share your hobby. Here, you can exchange knowledge and points of view about your favourite subject. Most chat rooms have specific rules of engagement that prevent people from being disrespectful, rude or offensive – and, who knows, you might even have to curb your own tongue if you choose to sign up to one!

- **Organize your paperwork.** Moving away from the Internet for a moment – which is probably not a bad thing, as it can be a very overpowering environment until you become used to its extraordinary characteristics and nature – you might choose to use your computer to organize your life in general, for example filing all your household inventories such as Christmas or holiday and birthday card lists in a spreadsheet or some other computer program. We will explore the full range of choices in this area later in this book.

An Introduction to Hardware and Software

Hardware – that's an evocative term, isn't it? At this point, your memory is probably conjuring up images of the ironmongers of your youth, which these days, of course, have largely been subsumed into the ubiquitous DIY sheds that we all religiously attend at weekends, like modern cathedrals. Software, well, what does that mean? Maybe in the good old days it was a word you equated with something you might slip into to feel more comfortable before bedtime … perhaps not, but it's nice to dream!

No, in the world of computers, like so many things, these terms have been appropriated to have completely different meaning. The hardware in your computer system is basically all the physical elements, as follows:

Central processing unit (CPU) – This is the very small, very high-tech semiconductor "chip" that acts as the brains of your computer. The CPU is stored in a computer tower – or sometimes in the body of the computer monitor and/or keyboard itself, as is the case with some Apple Macintosh computers and all laptops and notebooks. Basically, this is the engine of your machine.

Monitor – This is the screen on which you view all information on your computer. When you type into your keyboard, the words appear on your monitor's screen. Think of it like your television screen.

Keyboard – This is what used to be known as a typewriter! You input data using the keyboard, as well as many computer commands.

Mouse – The mouse is the little plastic or metal device with a pointer and buttons that you control with your hand and use to click on items on your computer screen. You can also drag the mouse to make text or object selections or to perform specific actions with it. Some mice come with electric leads, whereas many new ones are wireless and not directly connected to the computer at all.

Peripherals – These are the accessories that make your computer the all-singing, all-dancing clever box of electronic tricks that it is. Peripherals include speakers, web cams, a microphone and a printer. These may or may not come with your computer when you buy it, but the latter will be equipped with numerous "ports" in which to plug any peripherals that you might choose to buy subsequently. Having said that, as with the computer mouse, these days many peripherals operate wirelessly and do not need to be connected directly to the CPU.

The software in your computer is the collection of "programs" or "applications" that enable it to perform its myriad functions. If the CPU is the heart or engine of your computer, think of the software as the blood or oil. We will explore software in greater detail later in this book – particularly in Chapter 5, "Working with Software" – but for now, here are just a few basics to help you gain an understanding of the role that software performs in your computing life.

Pre-installed software – When you buy your computer, it will come with at least one major piece of software known as the "operating system". This is the computer program that allows all the other programs to run. Without an operating system – surprise, surprise – your computer will not operate! The most popular and ubiquitous operating system in the world of computers today is Microsoft Windows 7. This system runs the majority of the world's computers, although any computer made by rival company Apple Macintosh comes with its own unique operating system known as OS, and there are other options for a variety of purposes, such as the free system known as Linux. For the purposes of this book, we concentrate primarily on Windows 7, as it is this system that any computer you buy is most likely to run. You will generally find a variety of other software pre-installed on any computer you buy these days, which might range from games such as Solitaire, an electronic version of the old playing-card favourite, or basic photograph, video or music-editing software. Chances are that your computer will also come pre-installed with at least one Internet browser as well, at the very least.

Utilities – All computers come with a range of software programs known as "utilities", which exist to help your computer run more efficiently. These will certainly include basic antivirus software such as the Windows Defender program, which will help to protect your computer from unwanted intrusion by malicious computer "bugs" and programs known as "spyware". More on this later.

Software to buy and download – You can purchase any number of different software programs to run on your computer. These might range from financial management programs such as Quicken to the extremely popular word-processing and spreadsheet software package known as Microsoft Office. However, not all software is for accountancy and work! There are many kinds you can buy in order to pursue just about any leisure interest, from garden design to needlework. If you buy software in a box from your local computer store, the chances are that it will come on one or more discs (CDs or DVDs, just like those you run on your stereo or television), which might also have links to Internet-based websites where you can download more information or functions. Alternatively, you can purchase software directly online, by paying for it with your credit card and then downloading it securely from a website to your computer desktop. Once again, we will give you a lot more information on all this later on.

Uninstalling unwanted programs – Sometimes you will find software on your computer that is of no interest to you and which you know immediately you will never have any intention of using. For example, this might include violent or frequently plain cretinous computer games that are seemingly beloved by every child over the age of five years these days, particularly boys aged anything from 10 to 35 …! (And we use the term "boys" advisedly!) If this is the case, you can "uninstall" these unwanted programs, freeing up valuable storage space on your computer for material that you actually want. This will also help your computer to run better, as the less data a computer holds, the more smoothly it will run. Think of it like a car carrying less rather than more weight …

PC, Macintosh, Laptop or Notebook?

Well, if you are still with us, then it is getting close to the time when you must decide which kind of computer is for you. Of course, there is any number of different brands and specifications to choose from, and ultimately you must make those choices yourself, just as if you were buying a new car or dishwasher. However, here we at least seek to apprise you of the different types of machine that are available and the pros and cons of each. Think of this process in terms of that car we mentioned just now: what would suit you best, a sports coupé, a saloon, a hatchback, an estate or a four-wheel drive? It is this sort of range of categories that equally pertains in the world of computers.

PCs

The term "PC" originated in the very earliest days of home computers and stands for "personal computer". These are the most common and popular of all home computers. They are also known as "desktop" computers, which is probably a better description than PC, because they invariably stand on top of a desk. A typical desktop computer comprises a tower that incorporates the CPU mentioned earlier in this chapter, a monitor, keyboard and mouse. As we also mentioned previously, it might come with additional features such as speakers or other peripherals. The monitor, keyboard and mouse are normally all situated on the desktop, with the tower positioned beneath, under the desk. Having said that, some people prefer to have their CPU within immediate reach, on the desktop beside the other elements. However, the CPU tower will always take up a fair amount of space.

The advantages of PCs are:

• they are generally sturdy, fast and efficient.
• they usually come with a large monitor, or can be paired with one as you see fit.
• they are less expensive than other computers.
• they normally come with good-quality graphics cards, so are good for working with lots of visual elements.

The disadvantages of PCs are:

• they take up a lot of space.
• they are not portable.
• they are more prone to viruses than some other types of computer, particularly Apple Macintosh machines.

If you are looking for a machine that is relatively inexpensive, easy to keep maintained and up-to-date and will sit happily on a desk in your spare room or study for several years without too many complaints, then a PC is probably for you. As mentioned above, you will find that they come in any number of different specifications and prices, but as a starting point, head down to your local Currys or PC World and take a look at what's on offer. Alternatively, you could browse retailers' and manufacturers' websites on a friend or relative's computer. Sony, Dell and Toshiba are all good manufacturers to consider and all have extensive websites. You can also try the websites of the retailers mentioned above.

Macintosh computers

These robust, stylish and distinctive-looking machines were the brainchild of Steve Jobs, the CEO of Apple Macintosh, who died in 2011. Jobs started Apple Macintosh with a business partner in the late 1970s, working out of the garage of his house in California. By the time of his death, Apple Macintosh was a multibillion-dollar company, the second biggest in the world. This was in large part due to the iconic designs and unique functionality of Macintosh computers, which are widely known as "Macs" for short. You might also have heard of the distinctively named iPhone, iPod (a portable music device) and extremely popular iPad, which is a form of computing device known as a "tablet". Macintosh computers began life as business machines, favoured by graphic designers for their robustness, speed and exceptional ease of use. These days, they have something of a cult following and are used by all kinds of people. This book was written on a Macintosh! The advantages of Macintoshes are:

- they are well-designed and built machines that last.

- they have a unique operating system – OS – which is very easy to use.
- they are not prone to computer viruses and bugs – in fact, they are virtually virus free.

The disadvantages of Macintoshes are:

- they are relatively expensive.
- they will not run software that operates on PCs. Given the greater ubiquity of the latter, this can be a problem, although these days a Macintosh version of most software is normally available.
- they are compatible with fewer peripherals than standard PCs.

You can buy Macintoshes from any general computer store and the company has its own distinctive shops in a number of locations around the world. The cult following of the brand is such that it is even lampooned in a fortnightly cartoon strip in the satirical magazine *Private Eye*, so although these machines are unquestionably excellent, you might want to think twice before joining a technological clique with such an infra dig image!

Laptops

These are portable computers that, as the name suggests, sit on your lap. Of course they can also be operated from a desktop or just about anywhere else! Laptops will generally do anything that a desktop computer can do, but their unique selling point is their portability. The early versions of these machines were hilarious – great hulking beasts that were not so much portable as more like concrete blocks! However, these days these machines will genuinely sit comfortably on your lap, featuring screens that vary from about 13½in up to around 17in as a maximum. Laptops are popular with travelling business people for obvious reasons, and one might suit you if you have a fairly itinerant lifestyle or if for any reason you find it difficult to leave your chair or bed and move to a desk. Like PCs and Macintoshes, nearly all laptops feature disc drives, which means you can easily insert CDs or DVDs so that you can download software, listen to music, watch films and so on. Most laptops offer wireless connectivity, which means that you don't have to plug them in when you are working or playing on them. This naturally increases their portability, which is facilitated by an internal battery. However, this battery needs charging regularly by plugging it into the mains. Although these days most laptops offer several hours of battery life, some have as little as only two hours and need regular recharging, which can be a pain. The other downside of laptops is that they do not come with a mouse, but instead have a fairly fiddly touch-sensitive pad with which you operate the machine, alongside a conventional keyboard. This can be tricky and should be borne in mind if you have arthritic fingers or anything else that might affect your dexterity. You can always plug a mouse into one of the ports that you will find on any laptop. Even so, many laptops have small and awkward keyboards, due to their reduced size, and this should also be taken into account if you have hands that do not work as well as they once did.

The advantages of laptops are:

• they are small, light and highly portable.

- they are great for low-maintenance computing tasks and browsing the Internet.
- they are generally no more expensive than low- to mid-level PCs.

The disadvantages of laptops are:

- they do not come with a mouse and often have fiddly keyboards and touchpads.
- their batteries need recharging regularly.
- their monitors are smaller, so more labour-intensive work tends to be more difficult to perform on them.

Notebooks

These very small, light and extremely portable machines are essentially smaller versions of laptop computers. They are also known as "netbooks", because they are so often used to "surf" the Internet and the very smallest of them are known as "tablets", "palm pilots" or generically as "handheld devices", although some people would argue that these three latter terms all denote individual categories in their own right. Notebooks are cheaper than laptops and are becoming increasingly common. They are also quite a lot smaller than laptops, so once again, if you have problems with your hands or eyesight, a notebook might not be a great choice for you. The other downside with notebooks is that they do not have disc drives and generally have fairly short battery lives.

The advantages of notebooks are:

- they are inexpensive.

- they are incredibly handy and easy-to-use.
- you can literally take them anywhere.

The disadvantages of notebooks are:

- they have no disc drive.
- their screens and keyboards are very small.
- they have only limited battery life.

Questions to Ask the Salesperson

Right, you are nearly all set to head down to your local computer superstore to begin the daunting venture of buying your first computer! And we would recommend that you do this, rather than buying for the first time either online or over the telephone. If you have a reasonably computer-literate son, daughter, grandchild or friend – and if you are not too proud! – it is probably a really good idea to take them with you when you go to talk to the salesperson. However, before you do this, accompanied or not, you need to study the following questions and answers to understand exactly what it is that you are acquiring. These are the bare bones you will need to ask and establish when buying any computer. We could go on, but a decent salesperson will do that, so ask them to explain anything you are not clear about as rigorously as possible and do not take no for an answer!

Of course, there are a lot of other questions that you could ask your computer salesperson, such as how big is the monitor, which peripherals come with the standard computer, what software has been pre-installed and so on, but the list is fairly endless and varies from machine to machine. It is best to concentrate on the key elements outlined in the following pages and then simply ask your salesperson to elaborate on the many other features that the computer under consideration will doubtless offer.

THE KEY ELEMENTS YOU NEED TO UNDERSTAND WHEN BUYING A COMPUTER

Don't part with your cash until you have at least a rudimentary understanding of the following questions and answers and have asked your salesperson to explain them at a level of detail that you can comprehend!

- What is the operating system? We touched on this earlier. The operating system is the software that runs the entire computer. If you are buying a PC, laptop or notebook, you should look for Windows 7 Home Premium as the minimum standard. If you are buying a brand-new Apple Macintosh, ask the salesman what version of OS X is installed and ensure that it is the most up-to-date operating system available.
- What is the processor speed? Every computer contains a processor incorporated on a computer chip. The speed at which your computer runs programs or completes tasks is determined in large part by the speed of its processor. This is measured in gigahertz (GHz). The higher the measurement, the faster the processor. When you buy, go for the highest number/fastest processor that you can afford.

- How much RAM does the computer have? Once upon a time, people used to joke about machines being powered by mice running on wheels inside them. Well, given the power that many computers have these days, you might be forgiven for thinking that this term refers to a male sheep built into the CPU and working hard, but it doesn't! RAM stands for "random access memory", and is the memory required to simply access and run programs. You should look for a minimum of 1 gigabyte (GB) of RAM on any computer that you buy for everyday tasks. Again, buy the highest RAM allocation that you can afford.
- How big is the hard drive? The hard drive is the area of the computer on which your data will be stored. Like RAM, its capacity is measured in gigabytes. These days you should probably look for a minimum of 160GB hard drive on any computer for everyday work and play, although the size of hard drives does vary considerably from computer to computer. Once again, here size matters, and you should always buy the biggest hard drive you can afford.
- Does it have a disc drive? Also known as optical drives, these are little trays or slots in the side of computers in which you can insert CDs and DVDs for viewing or playing. You can also insert blank CDs or DVDs into these drives and record media stored on your computer for use on other appliances, such as your television or stereo. Any computer you consider purchasing should ideally include at least one optical drive that should be capable of both playing back and recording both CDs and DVDs.

- Is the computer fully Internet enabled? These days, this question is barely worth asking, because any new computer that you buy for personal or home use should be set up with either a cable or wireless connection to get you onto the Internet and all its associated email, and so on, without any difficulties. This is because this is the purpose for which most people buy computers these days, regardless of their age or status. However, it is worth asking if the computer you intend to purchase has a wireless connection, especially if it is a laptop or notebook, and ensure that the connectivity will be compatible with either the broadband or dial-up telephone line that you will additionally need at home in order to access the Internet. However, don't be blinded by science – as we say, this question and its answer should be a formality these days.

If you have any particular concerns or preconditions – maybe poor eyesight – then ensure that you cover these with the salesperson. Do not be afraid to ask questions such as "can the type size be increased on the monitor?" Remember, you are the customer, and even these days the customer should always be right …

The Buying Decision

If you like a bargain, then you are sure to find one when you are buying a computer. If you are fairly mobile and have some time on your hands, try going from shop to shop and comparing prices of the same models of computer in each different emporium. You will be amazed at the variance in prices and of the deals on offer – for example, in terms of the free giveaways of printers, speakers, headsets and other peripherals with which many retailers try to tempt uncertain punters. Make a shortlist of computers and deals that you find replicated in two or three shops and then, if you have access to someone else's computer, or a café or library with Internet access, visit those retailer's websites to compare the prices therein. Next, try some generic computer retailing websites and compare the prices there for a third time. Again, we guarantee you will be amazed by the results and the sheer variance in prices.

Shop around

So, armed with this knowledge, you can see that it pays to shop around when you are buying a computer. Computers are highly desirable items that are permanently in huge demand these days, and the supply of these machines always far outstrips that demand. This means that deals are plentiful and it will pay to take your time. For these reasons, the warranties that come with nearly all new machines are most impressive and should be carefully compared before you make your buying decision.

Do not be intimidated by any salesperson or by the self-conscious notion that because you are of a relatively advanced vintage people will assume that you know nothing whatsoever about computer technology. After all, at the very least you are now armed with this book! The salespeople you encounter will all obviously want to make a sale, but you will always have plenty of choice and they will not be desperate, because there are so many people out there wanting computers and so many of the things available!

If money is tight and following the advice given above does not in time yield the kind of deal you are looking for, then you might want to consider buying a used or refurbished computer. This is much like buying a second-hand car. You will be amazed at the bargains that you can find, but be careful to check the reputation and quality of the outlet that you select and be sure to purchase some sort of warranty to protect you, in the event that the used or refurbished machine you choose should turn out to be not quite such a bargain after all ...

Chapter 2

GETTING STARTED

Right, you have taken the plunge and bought your first computer. Congratulations! You are ready to join the ranks of the hundreds of millions of computer users who populate the world today. That might be a relief or it might be a daunting prospect – but whichever it is, just be careful how you choose to interact with them all in future!

Siting Your Computer

The first thing you need to do, short of actually taking everything out of the box and ensuring that it is all there, is to decide where you are going to install your computer and its various peripherals. With regard to the latter, you might have decided to go for a bulk deal which includes a printer, or conceivably one of the many two- or three-in-one machines that you can buy these days, which offer scanning and photocopying facilities as well as printing. Between the CPU tower, monitor, keyboard, mouse and printer-cum-photocopier/scanner, that's quite a lot of kit!

Additionally, you might have speakers, an extra stand-alone hard drive, or some other peripheral to take into consideration. Consequently, you are going to need a fair bit of room to accommodate all this new equipment. Of course, if you have opted to buy a laptop, none of this applies – and you will have the added advantage of not having to connect everything up and plug it all in. Having said that, you will still need access to a printer and you will have to plug the machine into the mains after every few hours of use in order to charge the battery.

The best place to install a computer and all the goodies that come with it is a study, if you have one. Alternatively, a spare room is a good option. If you are short on space, it probably makes sense to install your new equipment in the living room, but computers and their extras do have a habit of making rooms look like offices, so this might not be your preference. The other thing to bear in mind is that using a computer can be very distracting for anyone else in the same room who is trying to read, watch television, listen to music or simply commune with the cat!

Do not consider installing your new computer in the kitchen, as computer chips and the steam from boiled cabbage simply do not mix. Seriously, any remotely damp environment will not do your computer any good at all, so if you have a laptop, resist the temptation to take it into the bathroom with you, or the shed or greenhouse in mid-winter. Although they have come a long way in recent years and are considerably more robust than they used to be, computers are essentially very sensitive beasts that need plenty of tender loving care. If they are not designed to be portable, like laptops, they are best set up in a warm, dry, stable environment on a level surface where plenty of air can circulate. An unimpeded airflow is important as, rather like some cars, computers need air to move freely around their working parts so that they do not overheat.

Do confer carefully with other members of the household about where to install your computer and all its other bits and pieces, as it will require quite an investment in terms of living space. Once you have placed all the various components on or around the desk or table that you should select as a permanent home, you can begin thinking about hooking it all up together. Bear in mind that, once you have plugged everything in and got it settled in, the fewer knocks and bumps the equipment receives, the better it will work! If you think that the cat is likely to jump up and take an interest in your new speakers, keep the cat out of the room. Remember, you are dealing with relatively sensitive equipment.

Plugging It All In

Before you turn on your computer for the first time, you need to connect your monitor, keyboard and mouse. Your computer will come equipped with several types of connection port, though these days USB (universal serial bus) ports are easily the most common. Of course, you should follow the manufacturer's instructions that will come with your computer in order to set everything up, but as a rule you can follow these guidelines for connecting the various components:

- **VGA port** (marked "VGA in") – connect your monitor.
- **USB port** (branch-like symbol) – connect various USB devices, such as a memory stick or digital camera.
- **Parallel port** (often marked "printer") – for connecting a non-USB printer.
- **Audio** (three round plugs) – for connecting speakers.

If you have acquired computer peripherals with wireless capability, you will normally only need to plug in a small transmitter that links the various components together without the need for cables. This will generally plug into one of the USB ports on your computer and will in any case be accompanied by full manufacturer's instructions.

Once you have linked up all the various individual components successfully, you should plug them all into the mains electricity supply. It is usually best to do this using a multi-gang plug point adapter that has inbuilt "spike" protection, which means that in the event of an electrical storm or some other disruption to your electricity supply, your computer equipment will not be damaged by a surge or other abnormality.

Turn on the mains power and then activate the CPU tower, monitor, speakers and printer (if necessary) by pressing their "On" switches. Once you are satisfied that everything has turned on properly (power lights or displays will normally confirm this satisfactorily), you are ready to begin using your computer. Here, we are going to concentrate on what happens next with the CPU, mouse and monitor. Information on setting up your all-in-one printer/scanner/photocopier is provided in the next chapter.

Installing a Mouse

Now we come to one of the more interestingly named components of computing, the mouse. This is so-called because it does resemble the rodent of the same name, although it is usually made of plastic or metal and does not generally come equipped with fur and whiskers! (Having said that, there is no doubt that you can buy computer mouses that look just like the real thing ...) Of course, the typewriters of old simply had a keyboard and a carriage that you would bash with your hand each time it reached the end of a line. Computers differ in that they are operated by both a keyboard and a mouse. The mouse, in particular, obviates many of the physical actions that were required when using a typewriter keyboard in the past. When you move your mouse around on your desk, a corresponding mouse pointer/cursor moves around the screen of your monitor in front of you. In simple terms, you control the actions of that pointer by using the right and left buttons on the mouse. Computer mouses have four main functions:

- **Clicking** – This means pressing and releasing the left mouse button. You can click while in a document in order to move the insertion point, enabling you to decide where to type your next word. Clicking can also be used in various windows to select checkboxes or radio buttons, or to turn features on or off. You can also click on objects in your document – maybe a picture or a table of some description – selecting them by so doing.
- **Right-clicking** – If you click the right mouse button, Windows will display a shortcut menu that is specific to the item that you clicked. If you right-click the

Windows desktop, the menu that appears lets you choose commands that display a different view or change desktop properties.

- **Clicking and dragging** – To click and drag with the mouse, you press and continue to hold down the left mouse button and then drag the mouse to another location. This enables you to highlight text, move objects and generally make selections.
- **Scrolling** – Many mouse models come equipped with a little wheel on the top that you can use to roll up or down to scroll through a document or website on your screen. You simply roll the wheel down to move through pages going forwards, or scroll up to move backwards in your document.

All this probably sounds quite complicated, but believe us when we tell you that this is so much easier and more convenient than using a typewriter! You will be amazed at how quickly you get the hang of using your mouse in conjunction with your keyboard. If you become very proficient with the mouse, it will save you an awful lot of keystrokes, which could be a blessed relief if you suffer from arthritis or if your hands are at all stiff.

Pre-installed Software

When you turn on your computer for the first time, you will automatically activate the Windows 7 start-up sequence (or Macintosh OS start-up sequence if you have bought an Apple computer). Here, we are going to take you through the Windows 7 set-up process, as this is by far the most commonplace and generic.

Once you have activated the power button, the Windows 7 Welcome screen should appear. At this point, you might be invited to select a password. See the box below for full details on how to create a strong password that cannot be easily "hacked".

TIPS FOR CREATING A STRONG PASSWORD

You will be asked to create lots of passwords if you enjoy an active career as a silver surfer, for example whenever you open an online account with a retailer. In order not to become completely befuddled by having too many passwords, it is best to select one or two strong and memorable tags that you can use over and over again on the Internet. The key thing is to select words and numbers that will not be easily guessed by anyone else accessing your computer. Follow these tips for strong passwords:

- **Length** – your password should ideally use at least ten characters.
- **Strength** – in order to make your password strong and difficult to guess, mix up upper and lowercase letters, characters and numbers.
- **Obscurity** – don't use the names of your family, close friends or that of any business that you used to run in the past – anything that could easily be associated with you.
- **Protection** – whatever you do, don't leave bits of paper lying around with your password written on them as an *aide memoire*!
- **Regular change** – the more sensitive the information you seek to protect, the more frequently you should change your password.

When you have created and activated your password, Windows 7 will verify it and then display the Windows 7 desktop. The icons that appear on your desktop may vary depending on which programs your computer manufacturer has pre-installed. The best way to get to grips with pre-installed software is to click on each of the icons in turn and follow the Help menus that are built into the individual programs. There is more on this in Chapter 5, "Working with Software".

Creating your new user account

The first thing you need to do with your new Windows 7 operating system is to create a new user account. This is easily achieved, as follows:

1 Choose Start → Control Panel.
2 In the window that pops up, click the Add or Remove User Accounts link.
3 In the next Manage Accounts dialogue box, click Create a New Account.
4 In the following dialogue box, enter an account name and then select the type of account you want to create:
    • Administrator – with this type of account you can do things like create and change accounts and install programs.
    • Standard user – as a standard user, you can't undertake the tasks of an administrator.
5 Click the Create Account button and then close the Control Panel.

If you subsequently wish to make any changes to your
account, do this in the Manage Accounts dialogue box
that you accessed in Step 3 above.

Creating other user accounts

Once you have logged into Windows 7, you can create or
switch to another user account. This means that people
close to you can have their own account on your computer,
with their own dedicated personal settings. Follow these
instructions in order to set up a new user account:

1 First, save any open documents, close any open
  applications and then choose Start.
2 Next, click the arrow next to the button labelled Shut
  Down, in the bottom right-hand corner of the start menu
  and choose Log Off. Windows 7 will log off and display
  a list of users, if you have already created a/more than
  one user account. To log on again, click a user icon.
3 In order to create another user account, choose Start
  → Control Panel and, under the User Accounts and
  Family Safety heading, click Add or Remove User
  Accounts, then click Create a New Account.
4 Follow instructions to enter a name for the account
  and set a password for it, if you want to.
5 Once you have set up more than one user for your
  computer, before you get to the password screen you
  must click the icon for the user you wish to log on as.

You can also add photographs of yourself and any other
users for whom you set up accounts on your computer.
There is an Add or Change Picture option in the Add or
Remove User accounts area of the Control Panel.

Setting the date and time

Nine times out of ten, your new computer will come out of the box with the date and time already accurately set. However, depending on where your computer was bought or manufactured, there is a chance that it might be set to the wrong time zone. In this case, it is very easy to change the date and time so that they are correct.

1   If the taskbar is not visible, press the Windows key on your keyboard (the one with the Windows logo on it), in order to display it.

2   Right click the Date/Time display on the far right of the taskbar and then choose Adjust Date/Time from the shortcut menu that appears.

3   In the Date and Time dialogue box that opens, click the Change Date and Time button and enter new dates and times in the date and time fields as necessary. Alternatively, use the up and down arrows in order to change the time. Click OK.

4   To change the time zone, click the Change Time Zone button, choose another option from the Time Zone drop-down list and click OK.

5   In the new window, click OK again to apply the new settings and close the dialogue box.

Setting Up a Wireless Router

There is a fair amount of information about getting connected to the Internet and email in Chapter 7, "Welcome to the World Wide Web". If some of your basic set-up questions are not answered in the following few paragraphs, please turn to this chapter for further information.

If you are connecting to the Internet via a cable broadband or dial-up connection (although we emphatically do not recommend the latter, as it is very slow indeed), it should just be a case of connecting the telephone lead that comes with your computer to either the telephone point on the wall or the broadband home hub that you should already have installed. (BT and several other communications companies provide these when they install broadband at your home.) However, if you have bought a laptop or a PC which features wireless connectivity, you will need to set it up so that it can "talk" to your home hub. This is easily achieved.

When you first turn on your computer, if it is wireless enabled it will normally sense the presence of your router/home hub immediately, assuming the latter is turned on and working normally. Given that your telephone will already be connected to the hub, this should always be the case. Windows 7 will open a dialogue box that asks you if you want to connect to the wireless service on offer from your home hub/wireless router. All you then have to do is enter the password/number that is normally found on a sticker on the back of the home hub. Once you have entered the number or password, simply click OK and you should be up and running. If you have any difficulties at all, contact your Internet/broadband service provider (ISP) or refer to your computer's manual.

A wireless connection is normally very easy to achieve these days, so long as you already have broadband installed, because most people purchase computers with the primary aim of accessing the Internet. The process of getting connected has therefore been made as simple as possible within the last few years.

Setting Up an Email Account

Once you have connected to the Internet, whether wirelessly or via the conventional means of cables, you can set up an email account and begin telling all your friends about your new venture into silver surfer cyberspace! There is lots of information on email in Chapter 6, the evocatively titled "The Magic Caves of Email". Similarly, there is plenty of advice to get you started on using the Internet in Chapter 7, "Welcome to the World Wide Web". Here, we show you simply how to set up your first email account.

There are lots of different ways of opening an email account, and many online companies such as Google, Yahoo!, and AOL offer free services to which it is easy to subscribe on their websites. This means that you can set up several different email accounts and addresses at no expense whatsoever, which is a real boon if you plan to do a lot of emailing or run an online business of any kind. (You might not be thinking about the latter now that you have retired, but there is tremendous scope to start businesses online and you should not discount the possibility if you are feeling restless!) However, it's early days in your career as a silver surfer and we don't want to blind you with science, so here's how to get connected to the Windows Live email software that comes with your Windows 7 operating system.

1   When you first log on to your computer, Windows will
    open your default browser and display the Windows
    Live Mail Sign In window.
2   Click the Sign Up button and go through the series of
    simple prompts that comprise the Sign Up procedure.
    Windows Live will ask you to choose a username and
    password. For advice on this, see page 41, earlier in
    this chapter.

That's it. As simple as that!

Windows Live basic operations

There is plenty of information about sending and receiving
emails and attachments in Chapter 6, "The Magic Caves
of Email", but for now here is a brief introduction to
Windows Live and how to start sending and receiving
messages using this service.

When you access Windows Live Mail and many of the
other online email services, you are using a program that
is hosted online as opposed to software that is installed
directly onto your computer. The advantage of using one
of these services is that you can access your mail from any
computer, because your messages folders are stored online.
Conversely, if you use an email program such as Outlook
Express, the software and your messages are stored only
on your computer. In this event, you will be unable to
access your emails from other machines unless your service
provider offers an online remote access feature. However,
it is probably not wise to get into these kind of technical
realms until you are more familiar with your computer
and the ways of the Internet in general.

To send and receive messages in Windows Live Mail:

1 Use your browser to go to Windows Live – www.mail. live.com

2 Windows will open your default browser and display the Windows Live sign in window.

3 Click the Sign In to Windows Live button and enter your password in the field that appears. Next, click the Sign In button to sign in. Windows Live will then automatically send and receive all messages that you despatch or that have been sent to you.

4 Click the Mail link at the top of the page in order to view your Inbox. New messages will be shown with a small closed envelope icon and those with attachments will also show a paper clip icon.

Setting Up Internet Security Trial Periods

It is vital that your computer is protected from viruses and insidious "malware" from the moment that it is operational. We cover the thorny question of computer safety and security in exhaustive detail in Chapter 9, "Home Computer Safety and Security", and it would be a good idea to read this chapter sooner rather than later! However, at this early stage of setting up your computer it is sufficient to use the anti-virus and firewall software that will almost certainly have been pre-installed on your machine.

These software invariably offer free trial periods that you can take advantage of from the minute you begin using your computer. Some software comes free for an indefinite period and very often these will suffice in general terms. However, if you wish to protect your computer most effectively – and it is certainly a good idea to do this if you plan to roam cyberspace as a hobby – then it is worth investing in a more sophisticated version as soon as possible.

At the outset, we recommend that you try out one of the software that offers a trial period on your new computer. One software that is commonly offered to Windows 7 users is Bullguard. This firm generally offers a 30-day trial period with plenty of generous opportunities to extend this or invest in the full software through a variety of different payment schemes. In the long run, it will pay you to look into this or a similar software package.

Chapter 3

SETTING UP PRINTERS AND SCANNERS

Unfortunately not everything in the world of computers and the Internet is shiny, new and exotic. Like every other area of life, this realm has its mundane and particularly boring parts, and the process of setting up printers and scanners must surely qualify as one of these! For some reason, these peripheral devices often cause far more problems than the computer itself. We don't want to put you off, but this is certainly the case when it comes to installing printers, scanners or two- and three-in-one machines that will very often undertake photocopying as well. Any problems are probably due to compatibility issues more than anything – printers, scanners and photocopiers tend to be made by lots of other manufacturers than those who specialize in computers – but in terms of avoiding potential difficulties, sadly there are no hard-and-fast rules about which machines to buy.

With all of the above in mind, when you are purchasing your first computer it will pay you to have a lengthy chat with a friendly salesperson about the peripheral appliances that will work best with the machine you have selected. This way hopefully you will not encounter any problems, either during set-up or use, and you can sleep easy in your bed at night.

But why do we need printers and scanners at all? Well, although computers are amazing things, on their own they can only perform digital tasks. There are still plenty of occasions when you will need to turn digital files into printed documents and for that matter, printed documents into digital files. However, the computer can perform neither of these operations in its own right, so this is where printers and scanners come in. Photocopiers supply a sort of useful fallback position, in that they can be used to reproduce the product of a printer, whether the hard copy has come from a scan or another digital file.

In order to run either a printer or a scanner, you will need to install software in your computer that is known as a "driver". This will normally be supplied with the printer/scanner that you purchase, although on occasion you will be asked to download this from the Internet. Certainly, in the event that you upgrade your operating system on your computer at any time, you will have to resort to the latter course of action in order to keep your printer and/or scanner similarly up to date. Follow these steps to install a printer when using the Windows 7 operating system:

1   Carefully read the manufacturer's instructions that came with the printer you have acquired. Some printers need you to install software before connecting them, whereas others can be connected right away.

2   Turn on your computer and then follow the option
    below that best suits your requirements:
    • If your printer is a "plug and play" device, connect it
      and turn the power on. Windows will do the rest – it
      installs what it needs automatically.
    • Insert the disc that came with the printer and follow
      the on-screen instructions.
    • Choose Start → Devices and Printers.
    • If you have bought a wireless printer, choose Start
      → Devices and Printers and click the Add a Printer
      link in the window that appears. Choose the Add
      Network, Wireless or Bluetooth printer option and
      follow the instructions provided.

3   If you select the third option given above in Step 2, in
    the Devices and Printers window that appears, click the
    Add a Printer link near the top of the window.

4   In the next wizard window, click the Add a Local
    Printer option and then click Next.

5   In the Choose a Printer Port dialogue box, click the
    down arrow on the Use an Existing Port field and
    select a port, or just use the recommended port setting
    that Windows selects for you. Then, click Next.

6   In the next window, choose a manufacturer and then
    select a printer. You are then given two options:
    • If you have the manufacturer's disc, insert it in the
      appropriate CD drive now and click the Have Disc
      button. Then click Next.
    • If you don't have the manufacturer's desk, click
      the Windows Update button to see a list of printer
      drivers that you can download from the Microsoft
      website. Click Next.

7 In the resulting Type a Printer name dialogue box, enter a printer name. Then click Next.

8 Finally, click Finish to complete the Add Printer Wizard.

Setting a Default Printer

The chances are that you will only have bought and will use one printer, so in order to save you a lot of grief every time you want to use it, you can set up what is known as a "default printer" so that you do not have to go through the above process each time. Follow these simple instructions:

1 Choose Start → Devices and Printers.

2 In the Devices and Printers window, the current default printer is indicated by a check mark.

3 Right-click any printer that is not set as the default and choose Set as Default Printer from the shortcut menu.

4 Click the Close button in the Devices and Printers window in order to save the new settings.

There, that wasn't too painful was it? Hopefully your printer or printer/scanner will now work without any difficulties. You can set any number of preferences for its use via the Devices and Printers window in Windows 7, but it is best to have a thorough read of the manual that came with the printer you bought before you decide what is best for you. Every printer is different, of course, so we cannot go into specific details here.

If you ever want to remove a printer or simply upgrade to a new one, it is just a case of returning to the Devices and Printers window in Windows 7 and selecting Remove Device, once you have clicked on the name of the machine you no longer want.

Installing a Scanner

In order to install a "stand-alone" scanner, you will need to go through a very similar process to that involved in installing a printer. The first thing to do is to install your scanner driver software on your computer via the CD or DVD that should have been supplied with the scanner. Then, simply follow these instructions:

1   Connect your scanner to your computer's USB port. Read the manufacturer's instructions to check that you do this correctly.

2   Turn the scanner on. If your scanner is a "plug and play" device, Windows 7 should see it immediately and display a Found New Hardware message in the taskbar notification area at the bottom right-hand corner of the window. If this is the case, the scanner should then install itself automatically. If this does not happen, proceed to Step 3.

3   In the resulting Found New Hardware wizard, click Yes, This Time Only and then click Next.

4   If your scanner came with a CD, insert it into the CD drive and click Next. Windows 7 will search for your scanner driver software and install it.

5   Choose Start → Control Panel. In the search box,

type "scanners". Windows will return a set of links.
Click on the View Scanners and Cameras link. In the
resulting Scanners and Cameras window, click the Add
Device button.

6 In the next Scanner and Camera Installation wizard
window, click Next. You will be presented with a list
of manufacturers. Click the one that corresponds to
the maker of your scanner and then click the precise
model, which you should be able to find in the list on
the right.

7 Follow the wizard directions based on the model of
scanner that you chose in Step 6 and whether you
have a manufacturer's disc. If you don't have a disc,
Windows will help you to download the appropriate
software from the Internet. When you reach the
end of the wizard, click Finish to complete the
installation.

As with printers, you can modify your scanner settings as
you see fit once you have had a good read of the manual
that came with your machine. Again, Windows can help
you with this – you simply need to use the Scan Profiles
button in the Control Panel.

The principles of installing printers and scanners
in Windows 7 that are briefly outlined above apply
equally to a number of other commonly acquired
computer peripheral devices. For example, this is why
cameras are bracketed together with scanners in the
Windows 7 Control Panel. If in doubt, always consult

the manufacturer's instructions or seek advice on their website or the Microsoft website. With practice, you will soon get the hang of consulting websites for advice about computers and anything to do with them!

Chapter 4

COMPUTER CHALLENGES

Recently, as you have most likely entered your autumn years, it is possible that you have begun to find aspects of day-to-day living more challenging. Perhaps your eyesight is not as good as it once was, your mobility has been affected in some way or your hands are not as dextrous as they were when you were younger? We know that life has a disconcerting way of giving you the confidence and capability to do just about anything you want in middle age, only to snatch these attributes away abruptly the minute that you start approaching any status that might be deemed "elderly" ... such is life.

One of the problems that many older people encounter when they first begin using computers and the Internet is the regrettable discovery that these inventions have not really been conceived with the older user in mind! Consequently, the modern world of technology is bedevilled with impenetrable terminology, fiddly keys and switches, mind-bending graphics and frequently minuscule text. It's enough to send you screaming for the newspaper, television remote or other familiar, user-friendly totems of your past. Yet to miss out on computers and the World Wide Web would be to miss out on a lot of the best that modern life has to offer. For this reason, it is good to approach new technology with the attitude that you can teach old dogs new tricks after all, or at least show them ways to adapt old tricks that they are familiar with. The good news is that awareness of this problem has increased greatly in the last few years and computers in general have become far more accessible and easy-to-use. You will probably never become quite as proficient as your grandchildren at computing and general Internetry, or your children for that matter, but then after all they were raised with the wretched things! However, by following the advice in this chapter you should at least be able to rise to the basic physical and technical challenges that computers and the Internet present, and at the very least learn some tips and shortcuts for making your machine work the way that you want it to.

Coping with Jargon

If, by the time you read this chapter, you have just about had a sheep dip's full of RAM and your ADSL has been well and truly connected to your USB by your FireWire via some malware and a memory stick, you are probably beginning to lose patience with the extraordinary lexicon of terminology that computers and the Internet have spawned in their brief lifetime! Jargon is the only word for it. Never in the history of the world can one new technology have been responsible for quite so many additions to the English language. Whether it's "phishing" (a type of email scam) or "blogging" (posting on an online diary or journal), with everything from a "dongle" (a PC connectivity device) or a "Trojan" (disguised computer virus) in between, the language of this world courts confusion.

Although the World Wide Web was created by the thoroughly sane and down-to-earth Englishman, Sir Tim Berners-Lee, it is on the Internet that computer technology has become the most "geekish" and inaccessible. What's a wrinkly to do with something that seems to have been designed exclusively with Californian teenagers in mind? Well, the answer is to bust the jargon!

The glossary at the end of this book should go a long way towards helping you do this, and you will become increasingly familiar with computer and Internet terms the longer you use your new machine. However, the other thing that you can do – and this really is one of the marvels of the Internet – is get it to explain itself, quite literally! You can do this by simply keying the confusing term of your choice into any Internet search engine. The chances are that your enquiry will throw up at least a dozen different definitions, some more trustworthy than others. If in doubt, select one from a reputable online dictionary, of which there are many. A lot of these websites are run by the same venerable firms that produce the traditional printed versions of dictionaries, such as the Oxford University Press and Webster's, so you can certainly trust their information. Alternatively, simply access the following website, courtesy of the good old BBC:

www.bbc.co.uk/webwise/course/jargon/a.shtml

This will tell you everything that you will ever need to know about computer jargon. You need never be intimidated by it again!

A WORD ABOUT COMPUTER FILE SIZES

Computer file sizes tend to be one of the more perplexing issues for both the novice and older computer user. So, just what do all these file sizes and names mean?

Bit – The smallest unit in computing. It can have a value of 1 or 0. These days you would be hard pressed to find a file size listed in bits.

Byte – A (still very small) unit of information made up of 8 bits.

Kilobyte (KB) – A unit of approximately 1,000 bytes (1,024 to be exact). Most download sites use kilobytes when they give file sizes.

Megabyte (MB) – 220 bytes = 1,048,576 bytes or 1,024 kilobytes. This term is sometimes used to mean one million bytes.

Gigabyte (GB) – Approximately one billion bytes (1024MB). Most computer hard drive sizes are listed in gigabytes.

Here are some examples to show you how these basic units of measurement work:

- An old-fashioned 3½in floppy disk holds 1.44MB (1,474KB).
- A CD Rom holds 650–700MB (though most programs you get don't utilize the whole amount). This would be around 450 of those old 3½in floppy discs!
- A 20GB (or "Gig") hard drive will hold the same amount of information as 31 CD ROMs or 14,222 floppy disks.
- It takes between 10 seconds and one minute to download a 1MB (1024 KB) file using the average high-speed Internet connection.
- A typical page of text is around 4KB.

To see the size of a given file, just right-click it (in Internet Explorer) and select Properties from the resulting menu (or Alt+ double click the file).

Tools for the Visually Challenged

If your eyesight is failing you, there is no reason to discount computers from your everyday life, as these days there is a great deal you can do to facilitate their use with impaired vision. Windows 7 features a range of tools designed specifically for the visually challenged and you might be amazed at what you can now do to improve the situation.

To access visual tools in Windows 7, follow these instructions:

1   Choose Start → Control Panel.
2   In the control panel window under the Ease of Access tools, click the Optimize Visual Display link.
3   In the resulting Make the Computer Easier to See dialogue box, select the check boxes for features that you want to use. These might be:
    • **High Contrast** – Turn on higher contrast when left Alt+left shift+Print Screen Is Pressed. High contrast is a colour scheme that makes your screen easier to read.
    • **Hear Text and Descriptions Read Aloud** – You can turn on a Windows Narrator feature that will read on-screen text or an Audio Description feature to describe what is happening in video programs if you cannot see them clearly.
    • **Make Things on the Screen Larger** – if you click Turn On Magnifier, you will see two cursors on screen. One cursor appears in the magnifier window where everything is shown enlarged and one appears in whatever is showing on your computer. You can manoeuvre either cursor to work in your document.

- **Make Things On the Screen Easier to See** – With this feature, you can make settings that adjust on-screen contrast to make things easier to see. You can also enlarge the size of the blinking mouse cursor and get rid of distracting animations and backgrounds on screen.

4 When you have finished making settings, click OK to apply them and then click the Close button to close the dialogue box.

Making text larger or smaller

One of the biggest fears for computer users of the older generation is reading text that is very often so tiny as to be completely illegible. Even when you are equipped with your most powerful reading glasses, the type on some websites can be impossible to make out. However, once again Windows 7 comes riding to the rescue, as it contains a useful little feature that will enable you to make text larger or smaller as you see fit. You might not use the latter facility very much, but it's good to know that it exists! Here's how:

1 Choose Start → Control Pane → Appearance and Personalization. Click Make Text and Other Items Larger or Smaller in the resulting window.

2 In the next display window, click the Radio Button for the size of text you prefer. Smaller is the default, but you can expand text size to 125 per cent with the Medium setting and 150 per cent with the Larger setting.

3 Click Apply and then click the Close button to close the dialogue box. You will see the results the next time you log into Windows.

Tools for the Aurally Challenged

If your eyes have not yet given up the ghost, sadly maybe your ears have! In all seriousness, it is just as common to lose your hearing as it is your eyesight as you grow older. Of course you know that, and we don't want to state the blooming obvious. However, all is not lost and once again in Windows 7 there is quite a lot you can do to improve what is becoming an increasingly aural environment.

Sometimes Windows 7 prefers to alert you to events with sounds. If you are aurally challenged you might prefer to receive visual cues. Follow these steps:

1   Choose Start → Control Pane → Ease of Access and then click the Replace Sounds with the Visual Cues link.
2   In the resulting Use Text or Visual Alternatives for Sounds dialogue box, make any of the following settings:
    • Turn on Visual Notifications for Sounds (Sound Sentry) so that Windows will give a visual alert when a sound plays.
    • Choose a setting for visual warnings. These warnings basically flash a portion of your screen to alert you to an event.
    • To enable text captions for any spoken words, select Turn on Text Captions for Spoken Dialogue.
3   To save the new settings, click OK and then click the Close button in order to close the dialogue box.

If you are hard of hearing and can't always pick up system sounds alerting you to error messages, these visual cues can be very useful. The other thing you can do, of course, is simply to increase the volume of your speakers. You can do this by choosing Hardware and Sound in the Control Panel and then clicking the Adjust System Volume Link. Alternatively, you can use the volume adjustment in an audio program such as Windows Media Player, which is nearly always pre-installed on computers running on Windows 7.

Setting Up Speech Recognition

So, you have overcome the technical challenges imposed by the nuisances that are failing eyesight and hearing, but what if your hands don't work too well either? Sorry to keep going on about all these minor handicaps and impairments – sometimes it seems to be one thing after another as we get older doesn't it? Fortunately, however, even in the case of a distinctly physical handicap such as arthritis, once again Windows 7 can be of assistance. The best of these aids is something called speech recognition. If you find it difficult to type on a keyboard, you might prefer to speak commands, and the rather whizzy feature that is speech recognition will enable you to do this. Once again, simply follow these instructions:

1   Plug-in a desktop microphone or headset to your computer and choose Start → Control Panel → Ease of Access → Start Speech Recognition.
2   The Welcome to Speech Recognition message will appear. Click Next to continue.
3   In the resulting Microphone Setup Wizard dialogue box, select the type of microphone that you are using

and then click Next. The following screen will tell you how to place and use the microphone for optimum results. Click Next.

4   In the following dialogue box, read the sample sentence out loud. This enables the speech recognition software to begin identifying the unique characteristics of your voice. When you have finished, click Next. A dialogue box will appear telling you that your microphone is now set up. Click Next.

5   In the next dialogue box, choose whether to enable or disable document review. Document review allows Windows 7 to review your documents and email to help recognize your speech patterns. Click Next.

6   In the next dialogue box, choose either Manual Activation Mode, in which you can use a mouse, pen or keyboard to turn the feature on, or Voice Activation, which is useful if you have difficulty manipulating devices due to your arthritis or any hand injury. Click Next.

7   In the resulting screen, if you wish to view and/or print a list of speech recognition commands, click the View Reference Sheet button and read about or print reference information. Click the Close button to close that window and then click Next to proceed.

8   In the next dialogue box, either click Run Speech Recognition at Start-Up to enable this feature or leave the default setting. Click Next. The final dialogue box will inform you that you can now control the computer by voice and offers you a Start Tutorial button to help you practise voice commands. Click that button, or click Skip Tutorial to skip the tutorial and leave the speech recognition set up.

9   The speech recognition control panel appears. Say
    "start listening" to activate the feature if you used
    voice activation in Step 6, or click the Start Speech
    Recognition link if you chose manual activation. You
    can now begin using spoken commands to work with
    your computer.

Isn't that incredible ...?

Modifying Your Keyboard

Modern computers are incredibly versatile and there are
other things that you can do to improve life if you suffer from
arthritis, carpal tunnel syndrome or ulnar nerve damage. All
these conditions can significantly affect the dexterity of your
hands, as can the simple process of ageing, so the more help
you can give your mitts when you are working or playing on
your computer, the better! The first thing you might want to
consider doing is changing how your keyboard works. As
before, Windows 7 presents you with a positive smorgasbord
of option choices. This is how you access them:

1   Choose Start → Control Panel → Ease of Access and
    then click the Change How Your Keyboard Works
    link.
2   In the resulting Make the Keyboard Easier to Use
    dialogue box, take advantage of any of these settings:
    • Turn on Mouse Keys – To control your mouse by
      keyboard commands. If you turn on this setting,
      click the Set up Mouse Keys link to specify settings
      for this feature.
    • Turn on Toggle Keys – You can set up Windows 7 to

play a sound when you press caps lock, number lock or scroll lock, all of which you might do occasionally by mistake.

- Turn on Sticky Keys – This feature enables keystroke combinations to be pressed one at a time, rather than in combination. It's called "sticky" because it's as if the keys have been slowed down!

- Turn on Filter Keys – If you sometimes press a key very lightly or press it so hard that it activates twice, you can use this feature to adjust repeat rates to a different level. Filter keys will enable you to fine-tune settings if you make this choice.

- If you want Windows to highlight keyboard shortcuts and access keys with an underscore whenever these shortcuts appear, click on that setting.

- You can also use the Make It Easier to Manage Windows setting to prevent them from moving to the edge of your screen automatically.

3   To save your new settings, click OK and then click the Close button to close the Ease of Access Centre.

If, after making your desired changes things do not seem much improved, it might simply be that your keyboard is not very well suited to your hands. In that case, it is worth going to your local computer store and trying out a few possible alternatives. Some keyboards are designed for older or handicapped fingers, featuring larger and softer keys that are set further apart from one another, and so on. Ask your dealer for advice.

Customizing Your Mouse

When you first start using your computer, you might find that your mouse clicks, moves and presents the cursor in ways that do not entirely suit you. If this is the case, it is remarkably easy to make certain modifications, just as with so many other things in Windows 7.

To avoid having to click your mouse too often, instead of moving your mouse with your hand you can also use your keyboard to move the cursor. Alternatively, you can make a window activate by hovering your mouse over it rather than by clicking. Follow these steps to set up these features:

1 Choose Start → Control Panel → Ease of Access and then click the Change How Your Mouse works link. The Make the Mouse Easier to Use dialogue box will then open.

2 To use the numeric keyboard to move your mouse cursor on your screen, choose the Turn On Mouse Keys setting. If you choose to turn this feature on, click Set Up Mouse Keys in order to find-tune its behaviour.

3 Select the Activate a Window by hovering over it with the mouse checkbox to enable this feature. The name of the features says it all, really!

4 Click OK to save the new settings and then click the Close button to close the Ease of Access Centre.

If you are left-handed, you can improve life by clicking the Mouse Settings link in the Make the Mouse Easier to Use dialogue box and making the following changes. On the buttons tab, use the Switch Primary and Secondary buttons feature to make the right mouse button handle the usual left button functions such as clicking and dragging, and the left button handle the typical right-hand functions, such as displaying shortcut menus.

If you have difficulty seeing your cursor on screen, you can experiment with the Windows 7 colour schemes to see if another setting makes your cursor stand out better against the background. Additionally, you can modify the behaviour of the mouse pointer, to reset the pointer speed – that is, how quickly you can drag the mouse pointer around your screen. Do this by clicking the Pointer Options tab in the Mouse Properties dialogue box. Activate the Snap To feature that automatically moves the mouse cursor to the default choice in a dialogue box, or modify the little trails that appear when you drag the pointer.

Chapter 5

WORKING WITH SOFTWARE

Software is really the belt and braces of the computing world. Without it, hardware simply would not function – or to stretch the analogy, metaphorically its trousers would fall down! – and there would be no Internet. As we have already seen in this book, there are enough versions of software to turn our poor old minds inside out. However, although there are so many different programs, it is interesting to note that the word "software" is only ever used in the singular – there are no "softwares" in computing.

More on Operating Systems

As we saw in Chapter 1, "Choosing and Buying a Computer", the king of software on any PC is its operating system. For the purposes of this book, we concentrate on the world's most popular and ubiquitous operating system, Microsoft's Windows 7.

Windows has been around for quite a few years now and
Windows 7 is simply its latest incarnation. If you buy a
brand new computer, unless it is an Apple Macintosh,
the chances are that it will come with Windows 7 pre-
installed. However, if you opt to buy a used or refurbished
computer, it might be running an earlier version of the
system, such as Windows Vista, or Windows 7's immediate
predecessor, Windows XP. These two versions of the
system work in much the same way as Windows 7, which
after all is derived from these antecedents, and many
computers will still work perfectly well on these platforms.
The main difference is that, as these systems are older, they
do not come with as many features or, more significantly,
as many security tools. If you do run a computer on Vista
or XP, be mindful that you will need to update anti-virus
software, firewalls and so on even more frequently than
you would with an up-to-date operating system. The other
thing to bear in mind is that, while the contents of this
book are largely relevant to Vista and XP, the steps for
some common tasks in these systems are slightly different
from those for Windows 7.

There are three different versions of Windows 7, which is
designed for both home and business users.

- **Home Premium** – This endemic version of Windows 7
  is the system that you are most likely to find on your
  new computer. It is certainly the version you should
  go for if you are given the choice. Home Premium
  includes entertainment tools such as Windows Media
  Centre, designed for playing music and films. The
  system works well with design and image manipulation

programs such as Adobe Photoshop, which means you can do more than simply look at photos if you so desire. The other advantage of Home Premium is that it comes with a special set of features designed specifically for use with a laptop, including a battery power management system.

- **Windows 7 Professional** – This, as the name suggests, is the recommended version of Windows 7 for small businesses or if you work from home. If you are looking for really advanced security features, it might be worth spending a little extra and buying Professional.

- **Windows 7 Ultimate** – This is the top-of-the-range package from Microsoft, providing everything that Professional offers plus a few extra special security features, as well as some add-ons that means it handles languages other than English with particular proficiency.

It is your Windows 7 operating system that enables all other software on your computer to run. Now let's consider some of these other software and how to get the best out of them.

Launching a Program

If you want to work or play with any software program, you first have to "launch" it, in the typically grandiose terminology of computer world. Of course, it would not be enough simply to "turn it on" or "activate" it – no, you must launch it! Fortunately, this is easily done by any one of four different methods, as follows:

1   Choose Start → All Programs. Locate the program name on the All Programs list that appears and click it. Clicking an item with a folder icon displays a list of programs within it; just click the program on that sub-list in order to open it.

2   Simply double-click a program shortcut icon on the desktop.

3   Click an item on the taskbar. The taskbar should display by default. If it does not, press the Windows logo key on your keyboard in order to display it. Then click any icon on the taskbar, just to the right of the Start button.

4   If you have used the program you want recently and have saved a document, select it from the list of recently used programs that is displayed when you first open the Start menu. Then, simply click a document created in a program from the list that is shown. This will re-open the program.

Moving Information Between Programs

There will be occasions in your computing life when you wish to move data from a document in one program to a document in another. For example, imagine that you are compiling a letter in a word processing software such as Microsoft Word when you suddenly realize that there is a huge tranche of text in an email or some other document that is relevant to your letter and which you wish to include. Well, unlike the bad old days of typewriters, with a computer you can simply select the material that you want and then "drag and drop" it or "cut and paste" it into a document in another program without having to retype it all. Clever, eh? You can't do this with all programs, unfortunately, but many are sufficiently compatible to enable this incredibly useful feature. Here's how you do it:

1   Open documents in two programs simultaneously. Right-click the taskbar on the Windows desktop and choose Show Windows Side by Side.
2   If you don't need one of the active programs to be displayed, click the Minimize button so that just the programs you are working with appear.
3   Select the information that you wish to move and drag it to the other application document.
4   Release your mouse, and the information will be copied into the document in the new destination window.

You can achieve the same results by simply cutting and pasting or copying and pasting information from one application to another. To do this, first click and drag over the information in a document and then press Ctrl+X to cut or Ctrl+C to copy the item. Now, click in the destination document where you want to position the copied item and press Ctrl+V. It really is as simple as that …

Working with Files and Folders

Running a modern computer is really a bit like running an old-fashioned office. Whereas in the past in an office you worked with metal filing cabinets, cardboard folders and paper documents, now you work on a computer with a metal and plastic box, electronic folders and digital files. For Windows 7 basically organizes data in the same way that your office manager of 30 or 40 years ago organized the paperwork in the business you worked in. In computer software, you create files. These might be letters, emails, spreadsheets or any other sort of document, but they are all collectively known as "files". To keep these files in some semblance of order, they are then stored within named folders. These might be predefined folders or folders that you have created yourself. Sometimes, there is a need to create folders within folders – a bit like Russian dolls – in order to establish sub-categories of information to keep the filing system as clear and organized as possible. Then, ultimately all these folders containing files are stored on the hard drive of your computer. And it is not stretching the analogy too far to compare that hard drive with a big old metal filing cabinet that used to stand in the corner of your office …

Get the picture? We are sure that you do.

Creating files and folders

Creating documents and folders in computer software is easy. Here, we briefly explain how to create a document and folder in Microsoft Works, which is a basic word processing program that comes pre-installed on many Windows computers. You might find that it is available only on a trial period on your new computer, but if this is the case, it is very inexpensive to buy once the trial period has expired.

In order to open and save a new document:

1   Choose Start → All Programs → Microsoft Works and then select the Microsoft Works Word Processor.

The program will open and a blank document will be displayed.

2 Begin typing your text. Works, like all word processing programs, "wraps" the text, which means it automatically moves to the next line within a paragraph as you type. This is incredibly useful, and much easier than the old days of typewriters! You need to press Enter twice on your keyboard only when you want to start a new paragraph.

3 To edit the text that you have entered, you can click anywhere within it and press Backspace on the keyboard to delete material. Alternatively you can use the Delete key or click and drag material as you see fit.

4 To save the document, choose File → Save. In the resulting Save dialogue box, click the arrow on the right of the Save In field and click a different folder. Then, simply type a name for the document into the filename text box. Click Save.

When you click Save, the dialogue box will give you the option of creating a new folder in which to save your document if you so desire. You name any new folder in the same way that you name a file, simply by typing into the folder name text box.

Locating Files and Folders On Your Computer

Sometimes it can be easy to forget where you have filed or stored a document or folder on your computer. This has absolutely nothing to do with getting older – it is a common affliction of anybody who ever works on a computer! If you cannot find a file or folder, follow these steps to locate it:

1   Choose Start → Computer.
2   In the resulting Computer window, double-click an item such as a USB drive, a CD-ROM drive, or your computer hard drive in order to open it.
3   If the file or folder that you want is stored within another folder, double-click the folder or a series of folders until you locate it.
4   When you find the file or folder that you want, double-click it to open it in the application in which it was created.

Depending on how you choose to display files and folders on your computer, you might see text listings or icons. Some computers also provide thumbnail representations of file contents. You can use the View menu in the computer window to configure how to display files and folders to your personal preference.

If you are unable to find your lost file or folder by using the method outlined above, you can perform a simple search operation on your computer by following the steps below:

1   Open the Start menu and type a search term in the search box at the bottom.
2   A list of search results will appear, divided by the location of the results.
3   Click the See More Results link.
4   In the window that appears, click an item in order to view it.

5   When you have located the file that you want, you can
    double-click it to open it.

Of course, the ease with which you find files and folders
depends entirely on how organized you were about
storing them in the first place! Think back to that office
filing cabinet all those years ago. Were you scrupulous
about filing documents in the correct folders and sub-
folders? Could you always find what you were looking
for without delay? Did you pride yourself on your ability
to snap open the filing cabinet drawer and then pluck out
the relevant file for an expectant colleague while barely
having to look into the drawer? Well, the same applies
to your computer. If you keep lots of well-ordered and
clearly named folders on your hard drive, comprising
equally well ordered and named files, you will never
go too far wrong. Conversely, if your filing skills leave
something to be desired, you will probably spend a lot of
time using your computer Search facility!

Backing Up Files and Folders

Computer hard drives can and do fail on occasion, and
there are few things that will cause you more dismay than
losing your carefully crafted and stored digital data for
all time. The good news is that, these days, as computers
become increasingly sophisticated, it is usually possible to
retrieve data from a failed hard drive. This is a technical
process that will usually have to be conducted by your
local friendly technician or computer shop, who will
charge you a fee based on the amount of data that has to
be retrieved and how long this takes.

However, you can forestall this dreadful eventuality by keeping regular back-ups of all your important documents and data. You can do this in a number of different ways – by storing information on memory sticks, by uploading data to dedicated storage servers on the Internet or by copying it to a back-up hard drive. However, by far the easiest way to back-up your files and folders is to "burn" them to a CD or DVD.

Now, don't worry, by mentioning the word "burn" we're not inviting you to conduct some sort of latter-day conflagration of the books – it is just another one of those rather silly and melodramatic computer terms! "Burning" data actually means recording it on to another medium, in this case the CDs and DVDs that we referred to above.

This is how you do it:

1. Place a blank writable CD-R/RW (read/writable) or DVD-R/RW in your CD-RW or DVD-RW drive and then choose Start → Documents.
2. In the resulting Documents window, select all the files that you want to copy to disc.
3. Right-click the files that you want and then choose Copy to Folder.
4. In the Copy Items dialogue box that appears, click on the CD-R/RW or DVD-RW drive and click Copy.
5. Click the Close button to close the document window.

If you wish to backup the entire contents of the folder, you can simply click the Documents folder itself in Step 2.

Of course, there is a great deal more to organizing, storing and backing up your files and folders then we have space to cover here. However, if you follow the essential basic advice covered in this chapter, you should find that other tricks of the trade come to you pretty readily. The operating systems of modern computers are essentially very logical, so if you learn the steps for conducting one procedure, after a while you should find it fairly easy to emulate this procedure with slight adjustments in order to discover how to do other things. The more rational and uncluttered your mind, the easier this will be to achieve. One of the great things about being older and using computers is that it will force you to exercise your brain, in much the same way that playing chess or doing Su Doku puzzles will keep the old grey matter in shape. Put simply, the more you experiment with your computer and try different things, the easier you will find it to progress in techno-world.

Chapter 6

THE MAGIC CAVES OF EMAIL

Do you remember a time when everyone used to correspond regularly by letter with everyone else? Do you recall the contemplative, heartwarming pleasure of reading a handwritten letter from someone you care about and then sitting down to write them a fulsome reply? Maybe you are still fortunate enough to enjoy these simple delights. Perhaps you have older relatives and friends who still send you regular missives that plop onto the doormat when the postman calls, just as a personal communication should do?

Well, if that's you, these days you are certainly in a minority! Probably a very fortunate minority, as there can't be too many greater little pleasures in life than receiving regular correspondence from friends and family, but a minority nonetheless. For it is far more likely that most of the people you know communicate largely by email, and that the only stuff that comes through your letterbox these days is a tide of junk mail and irritating letters from the bank and the Inland Revenue. But what is all the fuss about email? And why is this chapter perhaps curiously entitled "The Magic Caves of Email"?

The Lowdown on Email

Email is a worldwide phenomenon that has existed in the public domain for no more than about 30 years. However, in that relatively short space of time, countless trillions of words have shuttled back and forth through the ether as people exchange these fleeting electronic missives. Like some digital modern Mercury flying on winged heels, emails ping across the stratosphere all around us at all times. Imagine if you could see these electronic messages flying through the air? All would be dark – you would not be able to see beyond the nose on your face, such is the multitude that are sent every single day!

So, we chose to entitle this chapter "The Magic Caves of Email" because there is something supernatural about this medium of communication, which lurks and flits permanently in the background of our lives, as if secreted inside some mystical, hidden caverns ...

Maybe these analogies strike you as a little far-fetched. However, if you stop and think about it, the whole world of email is pretty weird and wonderful. Just imagine ... you can sit down, type out a message, click a button – and seconds later it can be read by someone on the other side of the world. A few seconds more, and you could receive a reply from them. Incredible, isn't it? No wonder the days of the carrier pigeon are numbered! If you are to enter this world, it is as well to know something of how it works – the best way to play the game, if you like. For there is a definite etiquette in sending emails – both social as well as business – vested in how to compose them, what is acceptable to attach to them and, perhaps most importantly, in how to avoid emails that you do not want to receive.

Basic Email Etiquette

As with everything else in life, it is important to be polite in the emails that you send. We are sure that you concur, as someone who was doubtless raised with manners from the old school. Try these tips as well, before you start regularly despatching emails:

- **Grammar, punctuation, spelling.** We are sure we don't need to tell you, but this is important to get right. Typing an email, or a response to one you have received – as opposed to writing one – is no excuse for being sloppy with your grammar. It's very easy to confuse the message if full stops and commas aren't used correctly, and poor spelling and use of language leave a poor impression. It's bad enough living in a world where kids are regularly handed out GCSEs and A-levels without being able to spell, never mind properly educated seniors contributing to the problem!

- **Avoid long sentences.** Keep sentences to a minimum of 15–20 words. Email is supposed to be a quick and easy medium that requires a different writing style to long-hand letters. Also, as a general rule, avoid emails that are too long overall – if the recipient gets something that looks like an encyclopedia, they may not even attempt to read it!

- **DO NOT TYPE IN CAPITALS.** Emails written entirely in capitals are both difficult to read and can be misconstrued as "shouting", which is considered rude in the world of email. You don't want to enrage your recipient unnecessarily.

- **Answer promptly.** People send emails because they want quick responses – otherwise they would write a letter or send a fax. Make sure you answer all emails promptly.

- **Answer the question – and pre-empt other questions.** If you are responding to an email from somebody else, make sure that you answer everything in the original email. Leaving anything unanswered will generate more emails and cause frustration.

- **Abbreviations and slang.** Be mindful of using abbreviations and slang in your emails. Not everyone knows what they mean and your message may get lost in translation!

- **Active versus passive voice.** Try to use the active form of a verb rather than the passive. Example: "I will pass your offer on to my wife today", rather than "Your offer will be passed on to my wife today". The former is more personal and proactive – the latter is rather formal, old-fashioned and stuffy.

- **Credit card and bank details.** Whatever else you do, NEVER include your credit card or bank account details in an email, unless you are sending one via a secure form on a reputable, accredited website. Simply do not use email to discuss confidential matters. Emails are like postcards – they are not secure and potentially anyone can read them. You would hate to expose either yourself, your family or friends in any way via a misguided email.

- **TO:, CC: and BCC:.** Be mindful of putting everyone's email address in the "To:" field, even if you are sending a group of people the same response. This shows the recipient that you have also sent the same message to a number of other people and it also publicizes people's email addresses without their permission. Using "BCC:"(blind copy) can avoid this issue. Make sure that if you "CC:" (copy) someone on an email that they are aware of why they are being copied in. Do not copy people unnecessarily. It is annoying to receive dozens of emails that don't really concern you and equally annoying to feel as though you are not important enough to be in the "To:" field when it does concern you!

- **Don't email when drunk, tired, irritable or ill.** This might be stating the obvious, but it is not a good idea to email when you are in an altered state, very tired, angry or not feeling terribly well. Always remember that email is an instantaneous medium and that once a message has been sent it cannot be retrieved. Unlike an ill-tempered or ill-advised letter that might be left overnight on the kitchen table for posting the following morning, when you might think better of sending it, an email will already have been sent and received by the time you get round to regretting writing it in the first place ...

- **Read your emails before sending them.** It is very important that you take a few seconds to check your emails before sending them. You will be able to avoid most mistakes in grammar and spelling, and by reading the email through the eyes of the recipient, you should generally be able to head off any misunderstandings or inappropriate comments.

Composing an Email

We showed you how to set up an email account in Chapter 2. Depending on the email software that you opt to use, composing an email is as simple as filling out a few fields in a form. All email software basically works the same way, but for the purposes of this little lesson we will use Windows Live Mail, which is a software option that you will most likely find in your Internet browser.

1   Open Windows Live Mail in your browser (www.mail. live.com).
2   Sign in, using the password you selected when you set up your email account. Then, click the 'Mail' button on the Windows Live Mail screen, if necessary, to go to your inbox.
3   Click the 'New' button to create a new blank email form.
4   Type the email address of the recipient(s) in the 'To' field text box. If you want to send a copy of the message, click the 'Show CC and BCC' link and enter

an address in the CC or BCC field text box.

5   Click in the 'Subject' field text box and type a concise yet descriptive subject title.

6   Click in the message window and type your message. Don't worry about hitting the return button at the end of each line – the email software has an automatic text-wrap feature that does this for you.

7   Read your email through and check your spelling. Alternatively, use the spell check facility that is built into the email software. (However, bear in mind that this might be set up with US English ...)

8   Click the 'Send' button. A message will pop up confirming that your email is on its way!

Email Attachments

Whereas once upon a time you could only send short text messages by email, these days it is possible to attach any number of different things, from photographs to pieces of music, from personalized icons and stationery headers to documents of many different kinds. Of course, in all cases the item you attach must be digital in nature, so that it can be dispatched electronically. The other key thing to bear in mind is the size of the file that you append to your email. We briefly examined file sizes in Chapter 4, 'Computer Challenges', but you might need to refresh your memory by re-reading pages 62–63 if the following does not make much sense!

As a general rule, you should never attach a file of more than about 5MB to one of your emails. It all depends on the size of the email 'gateway' that your recipient enjoys, courtesy of their Internet Service Provider (ISP), but while these vary they tend never to be much bigger than about 7 or 8MB. If you send emails with attachments that are too large, they will simply be bounced back to you and your recipient will never receive them. If you are not in a position to check the size of your recipient's gateway, or they don't know it, then it is far better to remain within the 5MB limit specified above.

Here is how you actually append and send an email attachment:

1 As before, go to www.mail.live.com, sign in and click on 'Mail' if necessary. Click 'New' to create a new email message, address it and enter a subject.

2 Click the 'Attach' button.

3 The 'Choose File to Upload' dialogue box will appear. Locate the file that you want and then click 'Open'.

4 The name of the attached file will appear in the attached field text box. This indicates that it is uploading. When the first attachment has finished uploading, you can click the attach button again and repeat Step 3 as many times as you like to add additional attachments. However, be sure to remain within the 5MB or so limit discussed above.

5 Click the send button to send the message and its attachment.

If you have a folder of documents that you wish to send by email but its size exceeds the rough limits outlined above, you can always split up the contents of the folder and send it as attachments on several successive emails. The same applies to individual files. If you find they are too big to attach in one go, split them up into several different documents and simply explain to your recipient in a covering message that this is what you have had to do.

Spam and Junk Emails

As you become more proficient on your computer, the more time you spend online and sending emails the more you will begin to realize that you receive a great deal of junk email that you simply don't want. This electronic rubbish is also widely known as 'spam', and sadly it afflicts the Internet like bindweed, as certainly and as ubiquitously as any paper junk mail you have ever received through your letterbox.

The good news is that, just as you can mount a sign in your front door window saying 'No leaflets or circulars' (and we bet you have!), or phone a helpline to remove yourself from various mailing lists, in the same way you can set filters and blocks in your email software and on your computer in general that will significantly reduce the amount of spam and junk email that you receive. Depending on the email software that you use, this is normally quite easy to effect. Simply go to 'File' in the start-up window of your email software and select 'Settings' or 'Filters'. It is normally possible to designate a dedicated inbox to receive everything that your computer then 'thinks' is spam or junk mail, so that you have a chance to review its contents every now and again, in order to satisfy yourself that nothing has crept into your junk box that should actually have gone into your main inbox.

Email Fraud and Things to Avoid

Sadly, like every other walk of life, cyberspace has a criminal element. There are plenty of hackers and other invisible people out there who are as intent on robbing you and misusing your good name and financial information as any con artist or crook you might have met in real life. However, if you learn how to spot the various types of scam that occur online, you will go a long way towards steering clear of crime on the Internet. Try the following tips.

SPOTTING SCAMS

If you are on the Internet – whether opening an email, its attachment or simply browsing on a website – caution should be your watchword! Before you click a link that comes in a forwarded email message, or forward a message to others, ask yourself:

- Is the information legitimate? If in doubt, you can check out the provenance and legality of the email you that you have received on a variety of websites designed for the purpose, such as www.truthorfiction.com, www.snopes.com or http://urbanlegends.about.com
- Should I click the link? If an email or instant message asks you to click on a link but you are unsure whether that message is genuine, phone the company in question using a past statement or the telephone book. Don't use a telephone number posted in the email, as this might be a fake. Never, ever respond to a request

---

to input your bank account or credit card details. No reputable financial institution will ever ask you for this information by email. Do not fall for this most common of Internet scams!

- Should I download photo or video attachments? If the email you have been sent has a photo or video attached to it, exercise caution before you click on the attachment. If you know the person who sent the photo or video, it's probably safe to download it, but if the photo video has been forwarded several times and you don't know the person who sent it originally, be careful. This is because clicking on such an attachment might deliver a virus or some other kind of bug to your computer. Also, on an Apple Macintosh, never download an attachment that has a '.exe' suffix. These invariably spell trouble.

In addition to these questions, always think carefully before you forward an email to a friend or relative, and especially a group of friends. Observe the email etiquette outlined above, ensuring that you keep the email addresses of other people confidential by using the 'BCC' field as necessary. Finally, always think before you click! Doing so could save yourself a great deal of trouble ...

There is a lot more we could say about email, but the space constraints of this little book mean that this is not possible. However, suffice to say that it is a very easy medium to pick up and understand quite quickly. Begin by sending out a few emails to your friends and you will certainly receive replies. Read those replies and perhaps respond once more in turn, or forward the combined emails onto others who might be interested in them, while carefully bearing in mind the advice given above. You will soon get the hang of it. Don't be blinded by science, as email is probably the easiest aspect of the entire Internet to get to grips with and understand. Just because you are older, there is no reason why you should not become a maestro of the magic caves!

Chapter 7

WELCOME TO THE WORLD WIDE WEB

To many of us, the 'net' is something ladies might wear over their hair at night, or a useful object to drape over fruit bushes during the summer. By the same token, the "web" is where a spider lives or what you will see on an aquatic bird's foot when you are passing a contemplative half hour at the local duck pond. However, these days, you cannot really afford to be unaware of possibly – and simultaneously – the most important, wonderful, irritating and frustrating invention of all time: the Internet, aka the World Wide Web. But why is it all these things? Well, important, because it's so powerful; wonderful, because it offers such variety; irritating, because it contains as much junk as it does "good" stuff; and frustrating, because it doesn't always work the way you might like it to, which, if you have already done some Internet shopping or form-filling, you might know to your cost.

So, What Does It All Mean?

Computers court confusion at the best of times, with all their
unfamiliar technical jargon and fancy Silicon Valley lingo.
However, when you get onto the Internet, you really might
feel as though you have stumbled across some 16-year-old
Californian geek's fantasy naming game. It's as if us old
folks are deliberately being excluded from some weird and
wonderful "virtual" club for the young, in which "RAM"
couldn't be further from being a male sheep and "tweeting"
is most certainly not something you would associate with
the dawn chorus. So, to get you started and begin pulling the
cyber space dust from your confused old eyes, here's a crash
course guide to common Internet-related terms:

- **The Internet.** This is an immense network of
  computers that contains information and technology
  tools that can be accessed by anybody with an Internet
  connection – from a computer, mobile phone or any
  number of handheld devices (but probably not your
  TV remote or stairlift control pad).

- **The World Wide Web.** This is an unimaginably vast
  set of documents and digital data that are collectively
  known as the "World Wide Web", or more commonly
  just the "web", for short. It's time to forget about
  ducks and spiders ...

- **Websites.** These are sort of virtual building sites,
  made up of "web pages", just as a book is made up of
  individual pages. Websites can be purely information-
  based or host communication tools such as 'chat

rooms', interactive 'blogs' or 'discussion boards' that enable any number of people in any number of places around the world to"talk" to one another via text messages.

- **Online.** Whenever you access the Internet via your Internet connection, you go "online". To get around – or "surf" (oh yes) – online, you use a software program known as a browser. There are many different browsers available and they are all free. Internet Explorer is Microsoft's browser and other popular alternatives include Mozilla Firefox, Google Chrome and Opera. All Macintosh computers come pre-installed with a browser called Safari. It's an appropriate name for a tool which opens up all the wonderful variety and exoticism of the Internet – including any amount of information on wild animals, pith helmets and khaki suits. Go "on Safari" and – well, you probably get the picture ...

- **E-commerce.** You can buy, sell or bid for a wide variety of items – just about anything, really – in a global, comprehensive online marketplace known as the world of "e-commerce". The "e" in "e-commerce" originally derived from the word "electronic", although sometimes you may be forgiven for thinking that it came from the word "erotic" ...

- **Hyperlinks.** More commonly referred to as "links", these are text or graphics that are normally picked out in stand-out colours on a web page. You can click on links to move from place to place within a web page, on a website, or between websites. It's a bit like changing aisles in a public library – a link will take you to a new set of information. Once you have clicked on a link, it usually changes colour to show that you have followed the link.

The Internet for the Older Generation

We have deliberately tried to lace the above information about the Internet with a little gentle humour, because for anyone new to computers all this can seem very foreign and difficult to take on board. Having said that, we do not want you to feel patronized! If you are at all daunted by what you have read so far in this chapter, don't be. The Internet really is not as complicated as some people make it out to be, and just because you are a little older than the vast majority of its users does not mean that you are precluded from sharing in its incredible bounty. Plenty of older people browse the Internet, and there is even a name for them – silver surfers! Are you ready to join their ranks?

Why do older people not use the Internet?

It is true that people aged 65 and above use the Internet relatively little in comparison to other age groups – 14 per cent of people aged over 65, compared to 57 per cent of people aged 16 to 34. Although this is a personal choice for many, there are some older people who are restricted in their usage because of issues related to cost, the complexity of the technology involved and a sense that the Internet lacks relevance to their individual lifestyles. Although of course much credence can be given to the first two of these reasons, it would be mistaken of you to think that the Internet is not relevant to older people.

Enabling more people to use the Internet – whatever their age – and reducing barriers to its use is the challenge that we all face in a society that is growing more and more dependent on the World Wide Web. We must ensure that older people who want to use the Internet are able to do so, and that those who are unsure about going 'online' are shown the benefits which are relevant to the personal and social aspects of their lives. If this little book goes some way towards achieving this, and more specifically persuades you that the Internet is worth getting to grips with, then all of this will have been worthwhile ...

Benefits of the Internet for older people

As we saw in Chapter 1, shopping online can offer both convenience and cost efficiency, as well as providing the opportunity to shop around for the best deals. Many websites also offer free delivery, which can really benefit you if you have limited mobility or don't have access to a car – or if you are simply doing loads of shopping!

Many older people don't like the experience of shopping online, either because they see it as a substitute for physical activity and social contact or because they don't trust the security of shopping online. However, older consumers who do shop online can enhance their online security by following some basic rules (see page 113).

Looking up health complaints online is also a popular use of the Internet for older people. There is a wide range of sources offering health information online, although the validity of some websites can be uncertain, so it is important to check that you use only reputable websites that are recommended to you by your doctor or another health professional. If in doubt, you should always cross-reference information to be sure it is accurate.

Banishing fear of technology

If you have never used a computer before, it is perfectly understandable that you might consider your lack of previous experience with these machines to be an insurmountable barrier to the Internet. It is a sad fact that many younger people who have an Internet connection in their household may not use it because of a low level of technological competence, a lack of motivation or the opportunity to ask for help. In that case, how can the rest of us possibly expect to cope? Well, it really is not that difficult. This book is obviously a good starting point, and asking for help from friends and family will also help you banish any fear you might have of new technology.

If you do struggle with the advice that we give you here, you could always enrol on a computer training course. There are lots available and there is bound to be a suitable training centre somewhere near you.

Selecting a Web Browser

Right, now that we have got some of the preliminaries out of the way – and have hopefully reassured you a little into the bargain – let's get on with the practicalities of getting online. Or to put it another way, let's go silver surfing!

In order to access the Internet, you will require a telephone line. Ideally, this should be a broadband line which is permanently on, as this will enable you to surf and download material far more easily than a 'dial-up' connection via a standard telephone line. If you do attempt to browse the Internet with the latter, you will quickly become very frustrated indeed, as this is a terribly slow and inefficient way to go about things online.

The next thing you need to get online is what is known as a web browser. We touched on these earlier in this chapter, and you might remember some of the grandiose names that these tools always seem to have. For example, quite what "Mozilla Firefox" means is anybody's guess, but it is a very effective Internet browser!

Think of a browser as being a little bit like a telephone book. With the latter, you would find the right part of the alphabet and then use your finger or a pen to locate the specific name and address that you require. With a browser, you do much the same thing, instead tapping the name of the item you require into the window of your browser on the screen of your computer's monitor.

The chances are that your new computer will come pre-installed with a browser. If it is a PC running Windows 7, that browser will be Internet Explorer. Start by using this – it is a perfectly adequate tool – but if after a while you find that its features do not suit you for any reason, you could always download and try a different browser.

Setting Up an Internet Connection

To get going, the first step is to set up a connection in Windows so that you can actually access the Internet. Follow these simple instructions:

1   In Windows, choose Start → Control Panel → Network and Internet.
2   In the resulting window, click Network and Sharing Centre.
3   In that window, click the Set Up a New Connection or Network link.
4   In the Choose a Connection Option window, click Next to accept the default option of creating a new Internet connection. If you are already connected to the Internet, a window appears; click Set Up a New Connection Anyway.
5   In the resulting dialogue box, click your connection. These steps follow the selection of broadband.
6   In the next dialogue box, enter your user name, password and connection name (if you wish to assign one), and then click Connect. Windows automatically detects the connection and the Network and Sharing Centre appears with your connection listed.

And there you have it – you are online!

Navigating and Searching the Web

Now you can begin your adventure on the Internet. You should familiarize yourself thoroughly with your browser, and this will happen automatically with practise, but here is the essential information that you need to get going.

1   Open Internet Explorer by clicking the Internet Explorer icon in the Windows taskbar.

2   Enter a website address in the address bar. Start with Google, the world's most popular Internet search engine. Tap in www.google.co.uk on your keyboard. Then, press Enter.

3   Now choose any subject that you fancy, tap its subject name into the Google window and press enter again.

4   Select the website of your choice and click on its name. This will take you into the website.

5   On the resulting website, click a link – this will take you to another online page or document. Alternatively, enter another address in the address bar in order to proceed to another page. Note that a link can be either an icon or text. A text link is identifiable by coloured text, usually blue. After you click a link, it usually changes to another colour to show that it has been followed.

6   Click the back button to move back to the first page that you visited. Click the forward button to go forward to the second page that you visited.

7   Click the down-pointing arrow at the far right of the address bar to display a list of sites that you have visited recently. You can click on any site in this list and go directly to that website.

A couple of useful features are the Refresh and Stop buttons found at the right end of the address bar. These will help you navigate sites more easily. Clicking the Refresh button re-displays the current page. This is especially useful if a page updates information frequently, such as on a live sports page.

You can also use the Refresh button if the page does not load correctly; hopefully you will find that it does load properly when you refresh it. Clicking the Stop button stops a page that is in the process of loading. This is useful if you make a mistake when entering the address, or if the page is taking longer than you would like for it to load. You can always go back to it later, when it might load more quickly.

Customizing Your Browser's Toolbar

There are several things you can do to your browser's toolbar and general set-up in order to make navigating your way around web pages more easy. All browsers work in pretty much the same way, so the following advice is basically generic. Having said that, as before it is specifically based on the Windows Internet Explorer browser.

Using tabs

Tabs allow you to have several web pages open at once and make it easier to switch between them. A tab is a sort of window that you can use to view any number of sites. You don't have to create a new tab in order to go to another site. Having the ability to keep a few tabs open at a time means that you can more quickly switch between two or more sites without navigating back and forth either with the Previous or Next buttons or by entering new URLs. Follow these simple steps to create tabs.

1   With Internet Explorer open, click new tab (the smallest tab on the far right of the tabs).
2   In the new tab that appears, which will display some information about tabs, enter a URL in the address bar and press enter. The URL opens in that tab. You can then click other tabs to switch among sites.
3   Click the Quick Tabs button (it consists of four little squares on the far left of the tabs) to display a thumbnail of all open tabs. Alternatively, click on the Tab List button (the arrow to the right of the Quick Tabs button) to display a text list of tabs.
4   Close an active tab by clicking the Close button on the right side of the tab.

Setting up a home page

Your chosen home page will appear automatically every time that you log onto the Internet, so it is a good idea to choose a site that you like and plan to use regularly for this particular setting. A lot of people make Google their home page, simply because it is such a good launch pad to any number of other websites. However, the choice is yours. For example, if you have a share portfolio, you might want your home page to open a list of stocks and shares every morning so that you can check the progress of your investments. If you are really keen on knowing what the weather is going to do, you could always set your home page to a weather forecasting site so that when you turn your computer on in

the morning the first thing you will see is that day's forecast
This is how you set up a home page:

1 Open Internet Explorer and choose Tools – Internet
   Options.
2 In the resulting Internet Options dialogue box, on the
   general tab, enter a website address to use as your
   home page and then click OK.
3 Click the home page icon on the Internet Explorer toolbar
   (it looks like a little house) to go to your home page.

It is possible to have more than one home page, but this
is not recommended as it can become confusing. Having
said that, if you tire of your home page it is easy to change
it whenever you see fit by simply clicking on the home
button and choosing add or change home page.

Adding a website to favourites

If there is a site that you intend to revisit, you may want to
save it into Internet Explorer's 'favourites' folder, so that
you can easily go there again whenever you feel like it. It is
very easy to do this. Simply follow these instructions.

1 Open Internet Explorer, enter the URL of the website
   you want to add your Favourites list and then click Go.
   This is the button with two blue arrows on it to the
   right of the address bar.
2 Click the Favourites button to display the Favourite
   pane, and then click the Add to Favourites button.
3 In the resulting Add a Favourite dialogue box, modify
   the name of the Favourite listing to something easily

recognizable. If you wish you can use another folder or create a folder to store the Favourite in.

4 Click Add to add the site to your Favourites.

5 Click the Favourites button and then click the name of the site from the list that is displayed in order to go to that site.

You can organize Favourites into folders to make them easier to find. With Internet Explorer open, click the Favourites button to open the Favourites pane. Click the arrow on the right of the Add to Favourites button and then choose Organize Favourites. Here, you can create new folders, move, rename or delete Favourites as you see fit. When you have finished organizing your Favourites, click Close.

Viewing your browsing history

It can be quite easy to get lost on the Internet, especially if you visit many sites in one sitting. Obviously, listing and organizing your favourite websites will help in this regard, but you can also view your browsing history in order to find sites that you might have forgotten about and want to return to. Follow these instructions.

1 Click the Favourites button and then click the History tab to display the History pane.

2 Click the down-arrow on the History button and select a sort method. This will be one of the following:

   • View by date – sorts favourites by date visited.

   • View by site – sorts alphabetically by site name.

   • View by most visited – sorts with the sites visited most on top and those visited least at the bottom of the list.

• View by order visited today – sorts by the order in which you visited sites today.

3 In the History pane, you can click a site to go to it. The History pane then closes.

Customizing commands in the Internet Explorer toolbar

You can customize the toolbars that offer common commands in Internet Explorer so that the commands you use most often are included. Follow these steps.

1 Open Internet Explorer.
2 Click Tools → Toolbars → Customize. The Customize Toolbar dialogue box will appear.
3 Click the tool on the left and then click the Add button to add it to the toolbar.
4 Click a tool on the right and then click the Remove button to remove it from the toolbar.
5 When you have finished, click Close to save your new toolbar settings. The new tools appear; click the double arrow button on the right of the toolbar to display any tools that Internet Explorer cannot fit on screen.

Online Shopping

Now that you've learned the basics of how to get around the World Wide Web, it's time to have some fun! Depending on your gender, you may or may not approve of the fact that we have decided to start with online shopping ...

You can buy just about anything on the Internet and the tools that enable you to do this are becoming more and more sophisticated with every day that passes. The important thing to remember is that you cannot feel or see the quality of the goods online, although most retail websites now offer high-resolution photographs of all their wares.

The key thing to bear in mind when you are shopping online is security. Come to think of it, this remark applies to just about anything that you do online. When it comes to the Internet, caution should be your watchword. We don't say this just because you are older, this rule applies to absolutely everybody. Shopping online can be great fun, but it pays to exercise caution, much as you would do if you were visiting a market abroad for the first time.

As you gradually become accustomed to the Internet and its unique ways, you will doubtless become more adventurous. However, when you are starting out, it is safest to do your shopping with companies that you know and trust. Just about every retailer in the world now offers an online shopping facility, so begin by checking out the websites of a few of your favourite high street shops. Marks & Spencer, Tesco, Sainsbury's, WH Smith, Currys, Boots, Halfords and many, many more, all offer high-quality websites that frequently feature goods that are cheaper to buy online than they are in store. The other main advantage is that you can trust the reputation of these companies and buy with confidence.

When it comes to paying for goods, be careful to check how much you are expected to fork out for postage and packing, as this can be considerable. Then, before you enter your debit or credit card details online, be sure to satisfy yourself completely that the website on which you are shopping is totally secure, reputable and offers a secure method of payment.

Many retailers now insist on conducting all transactions via third-party secure payment systems such as PayPal to overcome precisely the kind of anxiety you might feel as you tap in your precious bank account details online for the first time. It will certainly pay you in the long run to sign up with one of these financial institutions (don't worry, this is easy as you will almost certainly be prompted to do so the first time that you attempt to buy something online from a reputable retailer), as they really do guarantee safety and security for your money on the Internet.

eBay and Online Buying and Selling

Not only is the Internet a great place to buy things, it's a fantastic marketplace for selling things, as well! If your days at the local car boot sale are well and truly over, or if you never really fancied that kind of environment in the first place, you could consider selling goods through online auction houses such as eBay, Craigslist or one of the many other similar virtual marketplaces that have opened on the Internet in the last few years.

eBay Inc. is an American Internet consumer-to-consumer corporation that manages eBay.com, an online auction and shopping website in which people and businesses buy and sell a broad variety of goods and services worldwide.

THE DOS AND DON'TS OF ONLINE SHOPPING

When you are shopping online:

- Do only visit websites that you know and trust.
- Do compare prices carefully in order to secure the best deals.
- Do check how much you are expected to pay for postage and packing.
- Do read the small print on the website very carefully.
- Do use PayPal or another secure payment system whenever possible.
- Don't fall for deals that look too good to be true – there will almost certainly be a catch.
- Don't buy goods from websites that you are not sure about.
- Don't buy goods from foreign websites unless you are absolutely certain, as delivery costs can be prohibitively expensive and you might be liable for import duty.
- Don't hand over your bank or credit card details unless you are absolutely sure about who you are giving them to.
- Don't forget to check out the terms and conditions of the deal, particularly those involving the return of goods that you are not happy with when you receive them.

Founded in 1995, eBay is one of the notable success stories of the dot-com bubble; it is now a multi-billion dollar business with operations localized in over 30 countries. You can find the UK version at www.eBay.co.uk. In recent years, eBay has expanded from its original "set-time" auction format to include 'Buy It Now' standard shopping and many other services. To give you an idea of the ethos of the company, its three principal slogans are as follows:

"Connecting buyers and sellers globally."
"What ever it is, you can get it on eBay."
"Buy it, sell it, love it"

Of course, you can buy anything here as well as sell it, so eBay is truly a fully interactive virtual marketplace. We do not have the space in this little book to give you a detailed set of instructions about how to hook up with eBay and the best way in which to use their services, but if this is for you then the best thing is to get online and have a close look at their website. You will need to join up, which will require registering, but you can read all the rules of engagement on the website prior to doing so. eBay is very well-established and entirely reputable, and you can rest assured that your money will be safe going through their hands. However, perhaps the key thing to bear in mind if you plan to use this website is that buyers of your own goods for sale, particularly for larger items, may expect to come and collect them from you personally at your home. By the same token, if you buy a large item from a private vendor, very often you will be required to go and collect it from their address. If this kind of interaction with strangers does not appeal to you, it might be better to consider buying or selling elsewhere.

TOP TEN WEBSITES FOR SILVER SURFERS

Here are our top ten website recommendations for older web users. These sites offer a mixture of things, from tailored advice for a better social life in later age to information for those who wish to work after retirement and directories of support in the community for those with a disability. Check a few of these out once you are online:

www.idf50.com
www.laterlife.com
www.saga.co.uk
www.silversurfers.net
www.sylviamilne.co.uk
www.ageuk.org.uk
www.seniornet.org
www.TheRetiredWorker.com
www.in-control.org.uk
www.shop4support.com

Social Networking

If you have teenage grandchildren, the chances are that they are addicted to something you might have heard of called "Facebook". Perhaps you have seen them with their faces buried in their laptops all day long, tapping away maniacally at their keyboards? Well, chances are they were "facebooking" with their friends. This Internet phenomenon is now so globally famous (or perhaps "notorious" is a more appropriate term) that a Hollywood film, *The Social Network*, was made all about its creation and establishment in 2010.

Facebook is a social networking service and website launched in February 2004. It is operated and privately owned by Facebook, Inc., which was founded by one of the brightest young stars of the Internet firmament, Mark Zuckerberg. As of July 2011, Facebook has more than 800 million active users. Facebook users must register before using the site, after which they may create a personal profile, add other users as friends, and exchange messages, including automatic notifications when they update their profile. Additionally, users may join common-interest user groups, organized by workplace, school or college, or other characteristics, and categorize their friends into lists such as 'People From Work' or 'Really Good Friends'. The name of the service stems from the colloquial name for the book given to students at the start of the academic year by some university administrations in the United States, to help students get to know each other. Facebook allows any users who declare themselves to be at least 13 years old to become registered users of the site.

So, what do you reckon? Is Facebook something that you might be interested in? It certainly has many members of a more advanced vintage and it is unquestionably a great way of keeping in touch with other people if you have many friends and relatives that are this way inclined.

There are other social networking sites out there, but Facebook has totally cornered the market in the last few years and if you are keen on the idea of this medium then this is really the only site to join. Your kids or their kids can probably tell you everything you need to know about Facebook if you are interested, but once again – a word of caution. It can be very easy to inadvertently reveal private details on this website so that they can be viewed by absolutely anybody on the Internet, anywhere in the world. We are sure we do not need to spell out to you just how potentially dangerous this could be ...

There have been countless horror stories over the last few years of unscrupulous people who have exploited Facebook users by accessing information about them under false pretences, and we would hate the same fate to befall you. You would not let a stranger into your home without proper credentials, so if you join Facebook or any other social networking website, you must be very careful to run your profile in such a way that a virtual intruder cannot gatecrash your life. The consequences could be disastrous. You have been warned!

Online Dating

Finally, in this brief introduction to the delights of the World Wide Web, a word about online dating. If you are a someone who is looking for love, the Internet could be just the place to do your looking. In all seriousness, this is one area in which cyberspace really does excel. If you have lost your loved one recently, or if you no longer feel disposed to meeting people in the conventional settings of parties, pubs, restaurants and so on, then registering with an online dating service and "meeting" people that way is a great manner in which to rebuild your confidence, check out potential partners' backgrounds and characteristics with more or less complete confidentiality and have some fun in the process. The real beauty of online dating is that all this can be done from the comfort of your own armchair, 24 hours a day!

If the idea of joining an Internet dating agency appeals to you, there are a number whose service is specifically dedicated to members of the older generation. You could start by trying out one of the following websites:

www.laterlife.com
www.midsummerseve.com
www.oldflirt.co.uk
www.ukmaturedating.com
www.seniorsdatingagency.co.uk

Happy virtual flirting!

Chapter 8

PHOTOS, MOVIES, MUSIC AND GAMES

One of the most amazing things about computers, the Internet and digital media in general is the way in which, in a matter of a few short years, they have completely revolutionized the worlds of photography, film making, music and video games. Once upon a time these areas of creativity were the exclusive preserve of a privileged few. If you thought about photography, for example, the hallowed names of David Bailey or Lord Snowdon would doubtless come to mind. Nowadays, though, it seems that every Tom, Dick or Harry has a mobile phone in their hand and is snapping away at the slightest thing. You have probably read in the newspapers, aghast, of unpleasant social phenomena that this digital ubiquity has spawned. Almost every day there are stories of dreadful "happy slapping" incidents, in which teenagers physically attack complete strangers and record the shocking results on the cameras and video recorders installed on their mobile phones. Similarly, you have probably heard of "revenge" postings of sex videos and the like on the Internet,

made by jilted lovers or spurned spouses. These are the
unfortunate downsides of such a world ...

However, enough musing about the decline of standards
in modern society! You probably have your own well-
developed views on these subjects without needing any
further provocation by this book ... Looking on the bright
side, there are many more positive applications of the
digital world to be enjoyed in the media on your PC, and
in this chapter we will show you how to make the most
of them.

Uploading Photos from your Digital Camera

If you enjoy taking photographs and have made the almost
obligatory transition from film to digital, you can upload
your images to your computer with great ease, where you
can edit and manipulate them with dedicated software,
share them online with your friends and family and store
them in Internet-based photo albums. Let's start with how
you get them on your computer in the first place.

- Getting connected – in order to upload photos from
  your digital camera, you must first connect it to your
  computer via a USB port. A USB cable will normally be
  supplied with the camera; it's simply a case of plugging
  the small end into the slot on the camera and the big
  end into any available USB port on your computer.
  Then, turn on your camera or change its setting to a
  playback mode as instructed by your manufacturer's

manual. Your computer should then be able to "see" your camera and will then normally open a software that is specifically designed to manage and edit digital photographs.

- Installing camera software – some digital cameras come with their own software that makes uploading photographs to your computer even easier. Install the software from the disc that will normally be supplied with the camera, and then follow the easy-to-use interface in order to upload photographs. If you find that software has not been supplied with your camera, you can simply connect your camera to your computer and use Windows Explorer to locate the camera device on your computer and then copy and paste photo files into a folder on your hard drive.

If all you want to do is print out your photographs, sometimes you can do this straight from the camera without having to upload your images to a computer. Some cameras will connect directly to printers, whereas many printers include a slot in which you can insert the memory card from your camera and print directly from it. This is a quick and convenient way of producing paper copies of your images, but if you value them it is probably a good idea to upload them to your computer in any case, by way of a back-up. This is because it is very easy to inadvertently "wipe" images from a digital camera's memory card and, like all digital media, sometimes these items can fail, which might result in the loss of your treasured pictures.

Viewing, Saving and Storing Digital Photos

Windows 7 comes with a handy piece of software called Windows Photo Gallery. Once you have uploaded your photos to your computer, it is easy to view them using this facility. Simply follow these steps:

1   Open Windows Photo Viewer and click Start → Pictures.
2   In the resulting window, if there are folders in this library, double-click on one to display files within it. Then, double-click on any photo in any Pictures Library folder. In the Windows Photo Viewer window, you can use the tools at the bottom to perform the following basic editing tasks:

- The Previous and Next icons move to a previous or following image in the same folder.
- The Display Size icon, which is presented in the shape of a magnifying glass, displays a slider that you can click and drag in order to change the size of the image thumbnails.
- The Delete button can be used to delete the selected image.
- The Rotate Clockwise and Rotate Counterclockwise icons will turn the image through 90 degrees at a time.
- The centre Play Slide Show button, which features a slide image on it, displays images in your picture folder in a continuous slide show.

Adding tags to photos

You can apply tags to photographs in order to organize and categorize them easily. To create a new tag:

1   Choose Start → Pictures.
2   Locate the photo that you want, right-click it and choose Properties.
3   In the Properties dialogue box that appears, click the Details tab.
4   Next, click the Tags item and a field will appear. Enter a tag in the field and click OK to save the tag.
5   Now, if you display your Pictures Library in Windows Explorer in a Details view, the tag will be listed next to the photograph. You can also view photo tags in Windows Media Centre.

Emailing Photos

One of the very best things about email is that you can attach photographs to your messages and send them hurtling through cyberspace to your loved ones and friends. This has to be so much easier than printing out photographs, pasting them into photo albums and then waiting months for your relatives to come round and share the pleasure of viewing them with you. Thanks to email, you can show friends and family your most recent images pretty much as soon as they have been taken. The response that you receive will be written rather than oral, but that is really the only downside! To email a digital photo:

1   Choose Start – Pictures. In Pictures Library, click to the left of the thumbnail in order to select the photo.

A check mark will appear in a check box to indicate that it has been selected. To select multiple images, click additional thumbnails.

2   Choose File → Send To → Mail Recipient. In the Attach Files dialogue box that appears, change the photo size by clicking the picture size drop-down arrow and choosing another size from the list if you wish.

3   Click Attach. An email form from your default email program will appear with your photo attached.

4   Fill in the email form with an addressee, subject and message, and then click Send.

Be careful to attach only small photographs to your emails, as larger graphic files might exceed the size of the electronic "gateway" of your recipient, in which case your images will not be successfully delivered and will come bouncing back to you.

Internet Photo Albums

As the Internet becomes increasingly sophisticated and more user-friendly, it is offering personal storage facilities for a variety of different media. The most commonplace of these are websites that allow you to store and post images in online photo albums. This is basically the digital equivalent of the physical photo albums that you have doubtless used for decades. The great advantage of these digital versions is that they can be shared by anyone who has a computer.

There are a number of different websites to choose from, some of which charge a subscription fee, whereas others charge according to the amount of digital space that you wish to rent. These days, some websites charge nothing at all and rely exclusively on advertising for their income. It all depends what you want to do with your photographs.

Flickr is one example of a website where you can upload your digital photographs by any number of different means and then share them with whomever you see fit. There is no charge to use this service, which has more than 60 million worldwide subscribers. These people are involved in ten million different special interest groups, and to date they have shared more than 5 billion photographs on the Flickr website.

Flickr is remarkably sophisticated, offering a range of highly developed privacy tools that mean you only share your photographs with the people that you want to see them. There is no hacking on Flickr! A multiple-backed storage system is designed to keep your photos safe and sound and a plethora of "apps" is available to enable you and other users to download and share images on any mobile device. However, we are getting pretty technical now, so it is probably time to move on! Seriously though, if the idea of storing and sharing your images online appeals, simply key "online photo albums" into your Internet search engine and have a good look through the multiple options that there are to choose from.

Playing Movies and Music with Windows Media Player

It is not only photographs that you can have fun with on your computer – there is plenty of scope to playback films and music as well! Incredible, isn't it?

Windows 7 features a wonderful piece of pre-installed software known as the Windows Media Player. With this exhilarating device, you can play back all sorts of different music and visual media to your heart's content.

To get started on working with music and movie files in Windows Media Player, simply follow these basic instructions:

1   Click the icon with an orange circle containing a right-facing arrow on your taskbar. Alternatively, open Windows Media Player by choosing Start → All Programs → Windows Media Player. If this is the first time that you have used the player, you may be prompted to make some basic settings.

2   Click the Maximize button in the resulting Media Player window. This is found in the upper-right corner of the window, next to the x-shaped Close button, and has a square icon.

3   Click Videos in the navigation pane to the left.

4   In the window listing video files that appears, click the Library folder that contains the movie you want to play.

5   Double-click a file to begin the playback. Use tools at the bottom of the screen to perform the following functions:

- Adjust the volume of any soundtrack by clicking and dragging the slider to the left, to make it softer, or to the right, to make it louder. Click the megaphone-shaped volume icon in order to mute the sound, and click it back on again as necessary.
- Pause the playback of the movie by clicking the round Pause button in the centre of the toolbar.
- Stop the playback of the movie by clicking the square-shaped Stop button towards the left.
- Skip to the next or previous movie by clicking the arrow buttons to the left or right of the Pause button.
- Click the Close button in order to close Media Player.

You will find that Media Player also includes rewind and fast forward tools for anything other than single movie clips. This will enable you to move around the on-screen movie in much the same way as you would control a DVD on your television set.

You can play music on the Windows Media Player by following the same basic instructions but just selecting Music instead of Videos at the outset.

Creating a Music Playlist

Like just about everything else in Windows 7, Media Player has fantastic organizational tools that will enable you to keep your online movies and music well-organized and easy to access. Perhaps the best of these tools is something called "Playlist", a feature which enables you to save a set of music tracks that you can create yourself, just like building a personal music album. You will need to upload all your favourite music to your computer from your CD collection first, but this does not take long and, once you begin enjoying the ease and convenience of Windows Media Player to play your music, you will wish you never had to bother with CDs in the first place. In order to create a Windows Media Player playlist, simply follow these steps:

1 Choose Start → All Programs → Windows Media Player.
2 Click the Library button and then click the Create Playlist button. A playlist appears in the navigation pane on the left. Type a name for the playlist and then click anywhere outside the playlist in order to save its name.
3 Double-click a category – in this case, Music – in order to display the libraries, and then double-click a library in the left pane. The library contents will appear. Click an item and then drag it into the new playlist in the navigation pane. Repeat this step to locate additional titles to add to the playlist.
4 To play a playlist, simply click it in the Library pane and then click the Play button.
5 You can organize playlists by clicking the Organize button and then choosing Sort By. In the submenu that appears, sort by features such as title, artist or release date.

Burning Music to a CD or DVD

We explained the origin of the computer term "burning" in Chapter 5, 'Working with Software' (see page 82). Just as you can save and store documents on CDs or DVDs, it is also possible to burn music or movies to disc. This is easily enabled by Windows Media Player. Simply follow these few easy steps:

1   Insert a blank CD or DVD suitable for storing audio files into your computer CD/DVD-RW drive.
2   Open the Windows Media Player, click the Burn tab, and then click one or more songs, albums or playlists and drag them to the Burn pane.
3   Click Start Burn. Windows Media Player will begin to burn the items onto the disc. The Status column for the first song title will read 'Writing to disc' and will then change to 'Complete' when the track is copied.
4   When the burn is complete, your disc will be ejected.

A Word About Playing Games on your PC

One of the most popular applications of computers for the younger generation is playing digital video games. These days, literally thousands of games can be downloaded from the Internet or purchased and uploaded from a CD or DVD. Some of these games are educational, but many of them tend to be either mindless, gruesome, intensely violent, plain unpleasant or all of the above. We think it unlikely that most contemporary games on the market will appeal to you and your generation – after all, they are primarily aimed at teenage boys – but you never know ... If this sounds like your bag, as with everything else it is simple to check out what is available online by simply being imaginative with your Internet search engine. Don't be surprised, though, if you find some pretty shocking material. You have been warned!

Alternatively, of course, you might enjoy traditional favourites such as chess, backgammon and draughts, all of which can be accessed and played online, along with popular card games such as Solitaire. In fact, many computers come with some of these harmless and life-enhancing games pre-installed.

Chapter 9

HOME COMPUTER SAFETY AND SECURITY

There is a good chance that you are probably bored rigid with being lectured by the younger generation about home security and watching out for yourself. Just because every now and again some poor biddy gets hoodwinked by some unscrupulous builder or other, and it makes the papers or *Watchdog* on TV, doesn't mean you are going to fall prey to the same kind of exploitation or danger. Nevertheless, there's always some well-meaning younger friend or relative bleating away about how you need to take better care of yourself and not answer the door to strangers and so on. All very tedious …

If you share this superannuated scepticism, then pay attention. For when it comes to computers, safety and security can and should not be stressed enough. This has nothing to do with your age or technical competence – *the following advice applies to absolutely everybody.*

Danger in digital shadows ...
Look at it this way. Whereas in the past you really
only had to worry about what was going on in your
immediate neighbourhood or the surrounding area – at
least in terms of the security of your home and your
family – when you are on a computer connected to the
World Wide Web, you should be aware that a potential
threat could come from just about anywhere. That bogus
gas meter reader standing on the doorstep translates
into literally thousands of computer hackers, charlatans,
thieves and general ne'er-do-wells on the Internet. This
is because your computer's/telephone line connection is
literally an electronic gateway to the entire world. When
you are online, just about anyone can feasibly "see"
you and get to you, in any number of unpleasant and
increasingly sophisticated ways ...

Now, we don't want to scare you half to death and put
you off using the wonderful universal tool that is the
Internet, but in terms of your computer and your online
connection, it really is important to batten down the
hatches and install digital security systems, just as you
have probably done physically around your own home.
The old maxim "better safe than sorry" applies more to
the Internet today than it probably has done to any other
walk of life in the past.

Understanding Computer Security

The key to understanding computer security is to appreciate that the software and files stored on your machine are vulnerable to attack in a variety of different ways. A threat to your computer security might come from a file that you copy from a disc you have inserted into your computer, but the danger is more likely to come from a program that you have downloaded from the Internet. It is very easy to do this completely inadvertently. The dubious or infected download might occur when you click a link, open an attachment on an email, or download a piece of software without realizing that what is known as "malware" is attached to it.

Malware is essentially dangerous computer programs, of which there are three basic types, as follows.

- **Viruses**. You have probably heard this term used in relation to computers, as although obviously it pertains primarily to illness, it was one of the first words to enter what is now the more or less inexhaustible lexicon of computer speak. A virus is a little program that is produced by the warped mind of some computer hacker (vandal) somewhere, who for whatever reason, is intent on spreading it around the Internet and infecting as many computers as possible. This might seem implausible to you – why would anyone want to do such a thing? – but unfortunately in cyberspace it goes on all the time. A virus can wreak all kinds of havoc in your computer, attacking data, deleting files, scrambling data or even making changes to the basic settings of your computer, which eventually cause the machine to grind to a halt and "die".

- **Spyware**. This, as the name suggests, consists of programs designed to track your activity on your computer. Yes, it is just as insidious as it sounds. Unscrupulous companies design spyware so they can figure out how to sell you things. Others will go even further and simply steal your passwords, enabling them to access your bank account and suchlike ...

- **Adware**. This is the computer equivalent of nuisance sales telephone calls. If you are unfortunate enough to download adware onto your computer, you will receive a series of irritating pop-up windows advertising a variety of products and trying to sell you things all day long. This is not good for your computer, as it will clog it up with unwanted data, thus slowing its performance dramatically.

The good news is that you can do something about all this insidious malware and carry on using your computer safely and securely. The most important thing to bear in mind is that you must regularly update the software that you need to install in order to counter these adverse viral programs. For the purposes of this chapter, our mantra is *update, update, update*!

Here's what you can do to stay safe and sound in computer land:

- **Anti-virus/anti-spyware/anti-adware software**.
  There are a variety of programs that you can buy
  to run on your Windows-based computer. Some of
  these programs are also available for the Macintosh
  format. They include Norton Anti-Virus from
  Symantec (below), McAfee Anti-Virus, or the
  freely downloadable AVG Free from a company
  called Grisoft. These packages will all help stop the
  downloading of malicious files and will delete any
  that they find on your computer's hard drive. If you
  buy one of these programs – and we recommend
  that you do, right away – *be sure to update it regularly*!

- **Windows Defender and Spyware Doctor**. These are
  two software packages that feature combined tools
  for detecting both adware and spyware. You can
  purchase Spyware Doctor from a company called PC
  Tools, whereas Windows Defender is already built
  into the Windows 7 operating system. There is more
  information on the latter later in this chapter.

- **Windows tools**. In addition to the proprietary software
  described above, there are a variety of other tools that
  you can download in order to keep your Windows
  software fully up-to-date with the latest security devices.

- **Firewalls**. Finally, computers can also be protected by
  the evocatively named software "firewalls". There are
  lots of different versions of these, designed for a variety
  of security purposes, and the one that is best suited to
  you will depend on the type of your computer. There is
  more information on firewalls later in this chapter.

TELL-TALE SIGNS OF A VIRUS ON YOUR PC

While it is a very good idea to run anti-virus software on your computer regularly whether it is misbehaving or not, there are a few things that you might notice going wrong with your computer which could indicate that unfortunately you have a virus. These are as follows:

- **Is the computer running very slowly?**
  If your computer is generally operating more slowly and takes longer to perform certain tasks, this is often an indication that you have a virus. Of course, it might be simply that your processor, RAM and hard drive are struggling because you have too much data on your machine, so this is not always the answer, but it can certainly be a clue to a more significant problem.

- **Have you recently downloaded a program from the Internet?**
  As previously stated, you need to be careful about which software you download from the World Wide Web. While many programs available on reputable websites are perfectly safe to download, some frequently "dodgy" items such as free screensavers, computer games and animated cursors will often contain hidden viruses or spyware. Sometimes you will notice a change in the way that your computer is operating as soon as you have downloaded and installed a new piece of software. If this is the case, use a previous "restore point" to return your computer back to a time before you installed it (see 153–154).

- **Are programs on your computer opening automatically or crashing repeatedly?**
  Some computer viruses are designed to sabotage programs. This can make them run in odd ways, automatically open without being instructed to, or refuse to run properly and then crash repeatedly. If this is happening on your computer, the chances are that you definitely have a virus.

- **Do unusual toolbars, homepages or links keep appearing on your screen?**
  If things keep popping up on your desktop that you are unfamiliar with or have not seen before, this is a good indication that your computer has been affected by spyware. This means that your computer activity can potentially be monitored by hackers, who could then copy your keystrokes in order to steal your banking passwords, etc., and raid your accounts. If in any doubt on this point at all, run anti-spyware software on your computer immediately.

- **Is there a lot of unexplained activity on your network?**
  If your modem or hard disc seem to be working all the time, or if the activity lights on your broadband modem are permanently lit up, these are good indicators that something unpleasant may have invaded your machine. Again, time to run the anti-virus software....

If any of these problems affect your computer, you know
what to do: simply follow the rest of the advice in this
chapter and ensure that your machine is fully protected
by up-to-date anti-virus, anti-spyware and anti-adware
programs.

Running Windows Update Options

The tools mentioned above that are designed for keeping
your Windows software abreast of the latest horrendous
developments in Hackerland are incorporated within
a generic tool known as Windows Update. As the
name suggests, this is regularly upgraded and will be
automatically downloaded by your computer, so long
as you are attached to the Internet via a broadband
connection.

You can control Windows Update yourself by accessing it
as follows:
Start → All programs → Windows Update

... and then clicking the Change Settings link on the left
side of the Windows Update window that appears. In the
resulting dialogue box, click on the Important Updates
drop-down list and you will find these settings:

- Install updates automatically – this does what it says
  on the tin!
- Download updates but let me choose whether to install

them – in this case, you are the boss. You choose when and which updates to install on your computer. The advantage of proceeding in this way is that you will not be interrupted by a computer suddenly deciding to conduct an update automatically when you are in the middle of an important piece of work.

- Check for updates but let me choose whether to download and install them – this option lets you know that the updates are available, but you can choose whether or not to install them.

- Never check for updates – this option is not a good idea, as it will leave your computer more at risk. You can always perform a manual update of a particular feature later on, which is the reason why this option is offered, but this is one occasion when it is better to let computer technology supersede human judgement!

In order to run Windows Update, simply follow these instructions:

1   Choose Start → All Programs → Windows Update.
2   In the Windows Update window, click Check for Updates.
3   In the resulting window, click the Updates Are Available link to see all optional or important updated links.
4   Select the links that you wish to update and then click OK.
5   In the Windows update window that appears, click the install updates button. You can watch the installation taking place on screen, after which short time you might be prompted to restart your computer.

As we advised earlier in this chapter, the key thing is to stay up-to-date. You literally cannot run Windows Update too often, such is the sinister proliferation of viruses and other malware on the Internet. It is a good idea to get in the habit of updating at the same time of day several days each week – or even every time that you log onto the computer, if you are not a terribly frequent user.

Setting Up a Password

To get away from all this digital technology for a minute, one rudimentary thing that you can do in order to protect your computer is to set up a password. This will prevent anyone else from accessing your machine. No one is suggesting that anyone in your family is about to log on to your computer and begin damaging your data, sending obscene messages or generally blackening your name, but it might make you sleep better at night knowing that if anyone has introduced something really horrible into your computer, only you can have been responsible!

It's easy to set up a password, as follows:

1   Choose → Start → Control Panel and then click User Accounts and Family Safety.
2   In the resulting window, click the Change Your Windows Password link. Then, if you have more than one user account, click an account in order to add the password to that account. Click the Create a Password for Your Account link.
3   In the Create a Password for Your Account screen,

enter a password, confirm it and add a password hint. (The latter is designed to help you stop forgetting your password, which might come in handy.)

4 Click the Create Password button.

5 You will now return to the Make Changes to Your User Account window. If you wish to remove your password at some point, you can click the Remove Your Password link here.

6 Click the Close button to close the User Accounts window.

You can change your password at any time by going to the User Accounts window and clicking Change Your Password. You can also change the name on your user account by typing Change Your Account Name.

Using Firewalls

If you associate the old term "smoke and mirrors" with your experience of computers to date, as might seem appropriate, the word "firewalls" could have a particular resonance. The drama of this term is so typical of computer programers and their acolytes. Everywhere in the world of computers you will find extreme or faintly melodramatic terminology: "hard drive", "RAM", "software", "malware", "FireWire", "Universal Serial Bus", "World Wide Web" – there is just something so self-important, so self-regarding about the digital world, rather like the grandiose fanfare that your computer doubtless emits every time you turn it on! Anyway, to firewalls, which are perhaps more evocative of Roman forts or mediaeval castles than they are a metal box with a screen attached to it ...

A firewall is essentially a computer program that protects your computer from the outside world. As we saw earlier, this is unquestionably A Good Thing, unless your computer is set up to run on a Virtual Private Network (VPN). You will need to check with your computer's supplier or IT advisor on this one, but suffice to say that using a firewall with a VPN will result in you being unable to share files and use some other VPN features. Having said that, chances are this is something you need not worry about.

You can purchase firewall software online and from any good computer store – try Currys or PC World. Firewalls come in a variety of different configurations and do vary according to the type of computer and the specification of individual models. Unless you are using your computer regularly for some specialist task, you probably do not need to bother investing in a specialist firewall. If you run Windows 7 on your computer, that operating system will already have a firewall built into it, as do many of the anti-virus and security software programs that were recommended earlier in this chapter.

Without wishing to blind you with science, installing an individual dedicated firewall might cause clashes with the firewalls already built into the software on your machine, so it might be easiest to stick with the latter at the outset, until you are feeling a little more technologically self-assured. If you do want to install a specialist firewall of your own, the small print on the software box will normally tell you everything that you need to know about potential clashes with Windows or commonplace anti-viral software. Whatever you decide to do, keep firmly in mind that the important thing is to have a firewall activated at all times and that it should be regularly updated.

Enabling the built-in Windows firewall

As with most features of Windows 7, it is easy enough to turn on the inbuilt firewall. Simply follow these instructions:

1   Choose Start → Control Panel → System and Security → Windows Firewall.
2   In the Windows Firewall window that appears, check that the Windows Firewall is marked as On. If it isn't, click the Turn Windows Firewall On or Off link in the left pane of the window.
3   In the resulting Customize Settings window, select the Turn On Windows Firewall Radio Button for Home or Work (Private) Network Location Settings and/or Public Network Location Settings and then click OK.
4   Click the Close button to close Windows Security Centre and the Control Panel. Your inbuilt firewall has been enabled.

Check Your Computer's Security Status

We really do not want to alarm you with the doubtless somewhat unsettling information comprising this chapter. However, as we stressed earlier, you really cannot be too careful when it comes to the safety and security of your computer. Remember: *update, update, update*!

So long as you do install and regularly upgrade anti-viral software and firewalls, you and your computer should not come to too much harm. However, if you fail to do this rest assured that you will soon receive a slew of advertising pop-ups and nasty little bugs that will undermine the smooth running of your machine. In this event, there is a distinct danger that many of your files and data will become damaged and there is even a possibility that your keystrokes might be tracked and copied in an attempt to steal your identity, or worse. If money is tight and anti-viral software is not top of the list when it comes to running your computer, consider using a gratis solution such as Spyware Terminator (see above), a "freeware" that can be downloaded from www.spywareterminator.com

Just as we do not want to worry you unduly, we also do not want to put you off using your computer regularly or in any way encourage you to become neurotic about its use. One way to reassure yourself about your computer's security status is to check it regularly following these instructions:

1   Choose Start → Control Panel → System and Security.
2   In the System and Security window that pops up, click the Review Your Computer's Status and Resolve Issues link.
3   In the Action Centre window that appears, check to see if the Security item states whether Windows found any anti-virus software on your computer.
4   If Windows does not find such software, click the Find a Program Online button and review Microsoft's recommended security software partners. If you want to purchase one of these solutions, click the logo of

the company that you wish to buy from and you will be taken to their website, where you can buy and download the software in question.

Above all, keep safe in cyberspace. It is always better safe than sorry …

Chapter 10

A HEALTHY COMPUTER IS A HAPPY COMPUTER

In a very short space of time, computers have become the most powerful and influential machines in the world. For many decades, it was probably the automobile that held this accolade, with its unparalleled diversity and ability to profoundly affect many people's emotions and excite their imaginations. Although the computer is clearly a very different kind of animal, which performs entirely different functions, somehow it has managed to insinuate its way into the public consciousness like no other invention.

It is probably due to the artificial intelligence of the computer, based on our own human intelligence, that increasingly we ascribe almost human characteristics to what are essentially plastic and metal boxes of electrodes and wires. Think back to the unsettling tale at the very beginning of this book – of the HAL 9000, the fictional killer computer that "stars" in Stanley Kubrick's *2001: A Space Odyssey*. Kubrick invested his computing creation with near-human "feelings" and qualities as long ago as 1968, so is it any wonder that we now treat computers with such awe, given that they have become so much more sophisticated since then? Maybe it is all simply to do with the faintly preposterous jargon and terminology that attaches to computers and everything to do with them, as we have remarked previously in this book. You are always hearing people talking about how their computer "has a virus" or "is dying", how it is "misbehaving" or "playing up", like a naughty child! Sometimes it feels as though the wretched things have completely taken over both the human race and the entire world ...!

However, you have doubtless been around long enough to know that this is really all just nonsense, and that what is sitting on your desk in the study at this very moment is actually just a lump of metal and plastic – a machine, and nothing more. Having said that, like all machines, your computer will benefit from regular tender loving care, over and above the meticulous observation of the safety and security advice given in Chapter 9. This final chapter of the book shows you how to keep your computer "healthy", and if, like so many people, you treat your machine like some strange avatar of your own existence, it might comfort you to think that by doing this you will also keep your computer *happy*. Make it an "OK Computer", to reference the title of a famous late 1990s' alternative rock album by the English band Radiohead, whose theme explores the social disconnection and dystopia that the universal domination of computers has in their view created. Whether you agree with them or not, it would be as well to follow the advice in this closing chapter and give your computer its best chance of surviving in an ever more diseased and corrupted virtual world ...

More About Backing Up Files

Earlier in this book we showed you how to back up your precious files to a variety of different media, from CDs and DVDs to portable hard drives and memory sticks. However, did you know that your clever computer can actually perform this task for you itself?

Backup software

Yet another ingenious feature of Microsoft Windows 7 is that it includes backup software as standard. This is an integral part of the operating system, called the Backup and Restore feature, which you can use to make copies of individual folders or for that matter absolutely everything on your computer, to guard against damage caused by a "crash". When your computer "crashes" (meaning "fails" – which of course it has to do as melodramatically as possible, in keeping with all other computer terminology!), there is a danger that your data can be lost or damaged, so it makes sense to use this feature at least once a week. You will need to have a backup drive attached to your computer in order to store the information you wish to replicate. This could be any of the stand-alone peripheral devices mentioned above and explored in more detail on pages 82. Here is how you use the Windows 7 Backup and Restore feature:

1   Click the Start button, then click Control Panel. In the Control Panel, click System and Security, and then click Backup and Restore.

2   Click Set up Backup. Follow the steps in the on-screen
    backup wizard. At this point you may need to enter
    your administrator password.

3   Windows 7 will now create a backup according to the
    settings you made during the setup. You may have to
    wait a few minutes for all the data to be backed up
    onto your backup storage drive.

You should set up a regular, scheduled backup when
setting up the Backup and Restore wizard. Windows will
then back up any new data you have added or any changes
to files onto the external storage device at regular intervals.

You can also create an "instant" backup, which overrides
the Backup and Restore schedule you have set and means
that you can "double-save" important new files that you
have created, whenever you feel like it. To do this:

1   Click the Start button, then click Control Panel. In the
    Control Panel, click System and Security, then click
    Backup and Restore.

2   Click Backup now. You may need to enter your
    administrator password at this point.

Restoring backed-up files
If your files have unfortunately been deleted, changed
accidentally or for any reason you need to restore the files
you have previously backed up, you can follow these steps:

1   Click the Start button, then click Control Panel. In the
    Control Panel, click System and Security, then click
    Backup and Restore.

2   Click Restore my files.
3   If you want to restore just a few files, click Browse for
    files or Browse for folders. Choose those that you wish
    to backup.

You can search for backed-up files in the Backup and
Restore panel. Simply click Search, then type all or part of
the file name, and then click Search again.

Creating a System Repair Disc

Do you ever experience "senior moments", when the old
grey matter lets you down momentarily and your memory
fails you, for no apparent reason? It's a nuisance isn't it,
but it seems to happen to all of us as we get older. Just
imagine if you could make a spare copy of your brain –
or at least your memory – that you could grab and refer
to whenever the one in your skull was playing up. That
would be handy, wouldn't it? Well, guess what – on your
computer, you can do exactly that!

In the event of something dire happening to your computer
– for example, some horrible malware attack, as described
in Chapter 9 – you will be thankful for having created
a System Repair Disc. This can help you fix Windows
7 if a major error occurs and can be used if you do not
have access to the Windows 7 installation disc or all the
other recovery options – such as a recovery CD – that
were supplied with your computer when you bought it. A
System Repair Disc can be created at any time. You will
need a blank CD or DVD in order to make one. Here's
how you do it:

1 Click the Start button and then click Control Panel.
2 Click System and Security and then click Backup and Restore.
3 Click Create a System Repair Disc from the option in the left-hand pane. At this point you may have to enter your administrator password.
4 Follow any on-screen instructions and insert your blank CD or DVD when prompted to do so.

There you are – it's as simple as that! Now, if you are unlucky enough to have to use your System Repair Disc – for example, in the event of a major crash and loss of data – follow these instructions:

1 Place the System Repair Disc into your CD or DVD drive.
2 Restart your computer by pressing the power button.
3 If Windows prompts you to do so, press any key in order to start the computer from the System Repair Disc.
4 Confirm or change any Language Settings and then click Next.
5 Select the Startup Repair option and then click Next.

... and Robert is the brother of your father, to coin a different version of a popular old phrase!

How to Restore Your Computer

Remember that spare, backup memory for your brain that we were discussing a little earlier? Well, let's take the principle one step further. Perhaps you or a loved one were unlucky enough to experience a mild heart attack, stroke, or some other age-related horror in recent years? In that case, just imagine if you could turn back time to just before that awful health event, when everything was working fine. As if it had never happened…. In virtual world, with the infinitely resourceful Windows 7 at your command, you can do exactly that to your computer.

The clever feature in question is called "System Restore". Essentially, after a major crash, it returns your computer system files and programs to a time when everything was working properly. You can also see which files will be removed or added when your computer is restored. System restore uses "restore points" that act like milestones for your computer. They can be created according to a specific schedule or prior to a major task, such as installing software. If necessary, you can then use System Restore to return your PC to how it was at the time it saved a "restore point".

Setting up System Restore

Before you begin using System Restore, make sure that you close all running programs and save all your open files. Once a restore point has been set, your computer will also automatically restart itself, so only start this process when you are ready.

1　Click on the Start button and right-click Computer. Next, click Properties in the pop-up menu that appears.
2　Click System Protection in the left pane.
3　Click on the System Protection tab and then click Create.

4   Enter a description, such as restore point "15 March
    2012", in the system protection dialogue box and then
    click Create.

A restore point will now be automatically created and
your computer will then restart. Once restarted, you can
use your computer as normal and, if you encounter a
problem, you can return your computer to the state it was
in at the time that you created the restore point.

It is a good idea to name your restore points fairly
accurately – ideally, not only with dates but with specific
times – so that it will be straightforward enough to know
which restore point you want to go back to in the event
that your computer crashes.

Using System Restore

If you do need to return your computer to the state it
was in at a previous restore point, then follow these
instructions:

1   Click on the Start button. Choose All Programs and
    navigate to Accessories, then System Tools in the menu.
2   Click on System Restore and then click Next in the
    Restore System Files and Settings window.
3   From the menu that appears, choose the restore point
    that you would like to return your computer to.
4   Click Next, then click Finish on the Confirm Your
    Restore Point window, in order to begin restoring your
    computer.
5   Click Yes on the 'Once started, system restore cannot
    be interrupted. Do you want to continue?' message.

Depending on how much data you have stored on your computer, it will probably take a few minutes for the restoration to occur. However, once Windows 7 has finished doing its thing, you should find that your computer has been returned to the state that it was in at the time you created your desired restore point. Now isn't that clever…?

If for any reason you wish to reverse the changes that System Restore makes, you can simply click Undo System Restore and follow the simple instructions that are given.

Do bear in mind that System Restore only affects Windows 7 files, such as system files, programs and other settings. Unfortunately, it does not affect your personal data such as email, photos and documents.

Checking a Computer Hard Drive for Problems

If you have read the advice given so far in this chapter, you will appreciate by now that computers running Windows 7 have quite extraordinary powers of self-diagnosis and recovery. Yes, with computers it's very much a case of "physician heal thyself"! in this respect, of course these machines are not very human at all…. However, it is clearly A Very Good Thing that computers can be kept so "healthy" these days by using all these various features. One of the cleverest features of all is that which enables you to check your hard drive for errors in order to help repair any performance problems, such as the machine working slowly. Simply follow these straightforward instructions:

1   Click the Start button, then click Computer.
2   Right-click the driver you want to check, then choose
    Properties from the pop-up menu.
3   In the Properties panel, click the Tools tab, then under
    "Error-checking" click Check Now. At this point
    you may need to enter your administrator password.
    The computer will now run a scan and will look for
    problems and errors on the hard drive that you have
    selected. If it finds and lists problems, you can attempt
    to fix them there and then.
4   To fix the problems with any folders or files that the
    scan reveals, simply tick "Automatically fix file system
    errors". Then click Start.

The quick scan described above won't necessarily solve all
your woes, but it is a good place to start – and certainly
quicker and cheaper than a trip to the local computer
shop! It is possible to perform a deeper check of the hard
drive, by selecting the "Scan for and attempt recovery
of bad sectors" option in the Tools tab under "Error-
checking". However, if your problem has not been
solved by this point, your computer might be in need
of some professional work. Before you resort to this,
though, do have a quick check of the advice given in the
"Troubleshooting" section on pages 163–165 of this book.

Recovering Deleted Files

Finally in this closing chapter, we explain to you the
incredibly useful feature that enables you to recover
files that you may have accidentally deleted from your
computer.

You can often do this by simply performing a few basic checks. Start by checking the Recycle Bin. This is usually located on the desktop. If you haven't entered it for a while, it is possible that the file may be in the bin and has not been deleted after all. To reclaim the file:

1   On the desktop, double-click the Recycle Bin and locate the file you need.
2   The file will reappear back in the location it was found in before it was placed in the Recycle Bin.

If you have followed the advice earlier in this chapter and have made lots of regular backups of your files, you can simply restore a deleted file from your backup. Do this as follows:

1   Click the Start button, then click Control Panel. Click System and Security, then click Backup and Restore.
2   Click Restore My Files, then follow the on-screen instructions.

You can also use the restore points advice that we gave you earlier to recover a file or folder that you have accidentally deleted from your hard drive. Follow these instructions:

1   Click the Start button, then click Computer.
2   Locate the folder that used to contain the file or folder that has been deleted and right-click it. Then choose Properties.
3   Under the Previous Versions tab, from the list of possible previous versions that appears, double-click a

previous version of the folder that contains the file or folder you want to restore. Then, click Restore.

4   Drag the file or folder to another location, such as another folder. The file or folder will then be saved to a new destination, ready for use.

And there you have it ... several exceedingly useful ways of recovering seemingly irretrievable situations. If only everything in life was so simple!

One final word of advice: as with everything else to do with computers, it is vital to keep your restoration software up-to-date, so that it can cope with any new problems that might be thrown up by your hard drive. You can do this very simply, by accepting the numerous updates that the Microsoft website will automatically despatch to your computer on a regular basis. Follow all this advice, and you will doubtless keep your computer as healthy and, as it might secretly feel deep down somewhere in its processors or electronic chips, as happy as possible ...!

ESSENTIAL SECURITY SOFTWARE

In addition to the security features that come pre-installed in your operating system, Windows 7, and the antivirus software that you should certainly invest in, there are one or two other useful bits of kit that you can download from the Microsoft website which will help to protect your computer from various threats. These are entirely free and are updated all the time, as they are designed to counter the constantly evolving tricks and subterfuge propagated by hackers around the world. They are as follows:

- **Microsoft Security Essentials**
  This free download from Microsoft helps Windows 7 guard against problems and dangerous software such as spyware and viruses. You simply download it from the Microsoft website, after which it will install itself and run quietly in the background, alerting you to any potential problems and malware and actively preventing spyware and viruses from entering your machine. This clever feature keeps itself entirely up-to-date from the latest security threats by automatically updating whenever Microsoft post a new add-on. In order to take advantage of this feature you will need to be running Windows 7, so unfortunately you will not have access to it if you are still on XP or Vista. You will also need a processor that runs at a speed of at least 1GHz, as well as 1GB of RAM or more and 140MB of free hard drive space. Needless to say, you also need a full-time Internet connection (via broadband), so that the software can keep itself up to date by

'talking' regularly to the Microsoft website. Download
Microsoft Security Essentials from www.microsoft.
com/security_essentials/

If you are interested in how Microsoft go about tackling
the threats posed to their operating systems, you can read
more about how this software works at www.microsoft.
com/security/portal/ This piece of advice is really only for the
more technically minded among you, though!

- **Windows Live Family Safety**
  If you have grandchildren who visit regularly and
  whom you allow to use your computer, you might be
  concerned about what they are able to access on the
  Internet. After all, as we have seen earlier in this book,
  not all is sweetness and light in the World Wide Web
  and there are plenty of sites that children are better
  off not seeing. The free-to-download Windows Live
  Family Safety is a useful addition to Windows 7 that
  will enable you not only to block certain sites but will
  also let you keep track of your grandchildren's online
  activities. If the latter feature sounds at all insidious
  or "Big Brother-ish" to you, you can always arrange
  the settings of the software so that it simply blocks
  rather than records activity. This "content filter" can
  be fully customized, allowing you to set different levels
  of access to various types of website. This means that
  you can prevent your grandchildren from accessing
  anything from violent computer games to hard-core
  pornography, with just about anything else in between.

If you do choose to monitor your grandchildren's surfing on the Internet, you can order "activity reports" through Windows Live Family Safety, which keep tabs on where they are going. This will then enable you to change settings from any location that has a computer connected to the Internet. You can also manage whom your grandchildren are contacting online by using instant messaging software and the safety features therein.

If you want to run Windows Live Family Safety on your computer, again you will need a 1GHz or faster processor, 512MB of RAM or more, a screen resolution of at least 1024 x 768, Internet Explorer 6 or higher, and an internet connection in order to download the software. You can download this free software from www.windowslive.co.uk/family safety.aspx

If you choose to install this software on your computer, it is probably a good idea to discuss its ramifications with your grandchildren's parents before you do so. Cyberspace is increasingly becoming a harbinger of family rows and disagreements!

Appendices

TROUBLESHOOTING

Computers can be temperamental beasts and will not
always work as they should – particularly if they have
been got at by something nasty on the Internet ...
However, before you tramp grumpily off to the computer
shop, try our top ten troubleshooting tips for silver surfers:

1 The computer will not start up
If your computer does not start as usual when you press
its power button, check that it is properly plugged in. Try
another electrical appliance in the socket to ensure that the
supply of power has not been interrupted by a blown fuse,
or something similar.

2 The computer screen is blank
If the screen is blank, check that the monitor is plugged in
properly to an electrical socket and that it is firmly linked
to the computer. Also, ensure that its power switch is on –
it can be easy to forget you have turned it off!

3 Problems with the video card

If the power indicators of the computer and monitor are on, and nothing is displayed on the screen, then there is a problem with the computer's video card. You should take your computer to the repair shop to have it replaced.

4 Windows 7 does not boot properly

If Windows 7 does not boot up in the correct way, you should reinstall the operating system with the Windows 7 bootable CD that was supplied with your computer.

5 The computer is on but not responding

If the computer is on but not responding correctly to keyboard operations, then it is said to be "held up" or "seized". In this case, press the power button continuously for at least five seconds; it will turn off and then restart your computer.

6 Software is functioning abnormally

If your software is responding in an unusual fashion, restart your computer and run a virus scan with a reliable anti-virus software installed on the computer.

7 Slow working computer

Computer performance can be improved by cleaning undesired files from the hard disc, getting rid of unnecessary icons on your desktop, installing a firewall, installing anti-virus and anti-spyware tools and undertaking frequent registry scans.

8 An external device is not working

If a peripheral appliance does not function correctly as you would like, turn it on as per the manufacturer's instructions and check that all connections are properly intact, the mains supply is working and you are following the prescribed mode of use. Also ensure that up-to-date drivers are installed and functioning correctly.

9 Internet network problem

If your computer cannot get connected to the Internet, check that network cables are connected properly, check the IP address, and make sure that your server or gateway firewall application is not blocking http requests from your PC.

10 Internet running slowly

If your computer is running slowly on the Internet, try deleting all cookies and temporary Internet files until the situation improves.

GLOSSARY

ADSL
Asymmetric Digital Subscriber Line. A Broadband Internet connection (3–200 times faster). You need to be close to a digital telephone exchange, on cable or have a satellite dish. You can remain connected permanently.

Advanced format
From 2011 hard disks were made to accept larger "sectors" (8x) than hitherto, increasing capacity and performance.

Adware
Advertising software that causes adverts to appear on your screen, either by invitation or (more likely) without your permission.

AGP
Accelerated Graphics Port. A more rapid connection (slot on the motherboard) for the (AGP) card which drives a monitor. Usually brown.

Anti-virus program
Something that can spot a virus attached to an email or already on your computer and deal with it.

Application
A program such as Word or Internet Explorer.
Applications almost always end in EXE.

AVATAR
A cartoon representation of someone in a chat room.
Origin: A Hindu spirit in human form.

Backup
Keeping copies of programs or work in a separate place in case of corruption of the first version. There are various methods.

Bandwidth
A measure of the maximum amount of data that can be transferred over the Internet or phone system at any one time.

Bit
Smallest unit of computer data. There are 8 bits to a byte

Bitmap
A graphic image which is made up of many tiny dots.

Blog, Blogger
A weblog or person who writes a website about what they do each day.

Bluetooth technology
Using radio transmission from your PC for controlling everything from printers to the lights, anywhere within a building. See also WI-FI.

Botnet
A group of PCs that have been commandeered by a spammer or other ne'er do well and used by them without the knowledge of the owners to spread mayhem around the Internet.

Broadband
High bandwidth Internet connections such as cable or ADSL for faster connections.

Browser
Program for browsing the Internet, e.g. Internet Explorer, Netscape Navigator.

Byte
A number of bits which make up a character, number or space on a hard, floppy disk or CD 8 bits equal one byte.

CAB file
A compressed file. In Windows they contain all the files necessary to create the Windows Operating System.

Cache
This is a general term meaning a section of memory.

Cookie
A small text file which is downloaded to your computer

without you knowing anything about it. Mainly they are used to trace your activities for marketing purposes.

CD/CDROM/CD-R/CDRW
Compact Disk Read Only Memory. Not really memory like RAM. They are the familiar discs on which programs arrive. They are Read Only because the tracks are "burnt" in and cannot be changed. The RW type can be rewritten to many times but cannot be read on another machine, so they are less useful for safe backup.

Chip
Silicon chip. The silicon base used to mount the millions of components that go to make up a computer processor.

Control panel
An important set of icons which allows you to configure the basic functions of your computer.

Control key
Marked Ctrl on the keyboard. Like Alt and Function keys, its use can vary from program to program.

Cut or copy and paste
Most Windows programs allow you to cut or copy a selected item (text or picture) and paste it into another place or even another program. So you can copy a picture from one program and paste it into another.

Database
A list of items of data kept on a computer disc so it can be amended, searched or printed.

Desktop
The main, first page in Windows.

Digital
The method of storing or transmitting things as a series of numbers.

DOS
Disk Operating System. The original Operating System used on PCs without which the machine would be a just a collection of useless electronic parts. Gradually being superseded by Windows.

DOS exploit
This is a very different DOS, meaning Denial Of Service. The term is used when your anti-spyware software finds something on your PC that indicates your PC is infected by a virus which will make your PC, along with millions of others, contact a major computer, causing that computer to seize up.

Download
The process of transferring files such as pictures, text or programs from the web to your machine's hard drive.

DPI
Dots per inch. Used in connection with printers, scanners and monitors.

Drag and drop
The facility in most programs to select text or a file and drag it to another position.

Driver
Software that enables certain peripherals to work, e.g. printer, sound card, camera.

Drop down menu
When you click a menu item at the top a series of sub-menus is revealed.

DTP
Desktop Publishing. Creating print-ready documents on a computer.

Dual core Processor
Like two computers on one silicon chip, thus able to take on more jobs at the same time.

DVD-ROM
Digital Versatile Disc Read Only Memory. A disc capable of containing much more than a CD Used for music, films and big programs.

DVD-RW
A rewriteable DVD.

DVD Player – Special disc player for DVD disks. Capable of playing CDs as well

E-book
Electronic book.

E-BAY
The most popular online auction site.

E-commerce
Business conducted over the Internet.

Express card
The latest, fastest adapter being fitted to laptops in place of the PCMCIA card. It will enable fast data transfer for many peripherals.

Ezine
Online magazine.

Email
Messages sent to people over the Internet. Email addresses always contain the symbol @ somewhere.

Email client
Program you use to send and receive emails Outlook Express, Eudora, Netscape Communicator.

Favourites
Or bookmarks. All web browsers enable you to add favourite sites to a list for easy retrieval.

Firewall
A program that ensures that your PC has no open "ports" which allow hackers to access it.

FireWire
A socket on some PCs that enables 50MB/second transfer of data faster than via Serial, Parallel and 30 times faster than a USB 1.1 port.

Floppy disk
Hardly floppy these days! 3½in discs you can use to save data so you can copy it to and from your hard disc.

FLV format
Stands for Flash Video. This is a highly compressed video format and is commonly used by the BBC and YouTube sites.

Font
A collection of characters of a predefined style, such as Times or Arial.

Function keys
Programable keys F1 to F12, which may vary in their use.

Geek
Someone obsessed with computers.

Gigabyre
A thousand million bytes.

Gigahertz
A thousand megahertz.

Graphics
The general term used for pictures and drawings.

Graphics card
The part of the PC that sends signals to the monitor or display.

Hacker
A person who breaks into other people's computers.

Hard disk
A set of spinning disks coated with recording material.
Can retain details of programs and data indefinitely.

Hardware
Any piece of equipment such as the computer or a printer.

HD-DVD
One of two new DVD standards which use blue lasers. See
also Blu-ray.

Home page
The first page of a website, usually Index.htm.

Hotmail
It is possible to get an email address before you get a
computer and pick up mail at a cybercafe. It might take
the form of Yourname@hotmail.com.

Hypertext links
These are the addresses of websites or pages, which can be
anywhere in the world. They are usually coloured blue and
are underlined. When the cursor arrow hovers over one it
will change its shape to show it is a link.

Icon
A graphic representation of something such as a shortcut
to a program or a religious picture or other form of
representation.

IM
Instant Messaging. Text based messages to people online, using Microsoft or AOL Instant Messenger.

Inkjet or Bubblejet Printer
The commonest form of printer which squirts ink onto the paper.

Internet
A conglomeration of linked computers which can be accessed by people who are connected to the "web".

Internet explorer
The main web browser, issued free by Microsoft. The other is Netscape Navigator.

iPod
Apple's tiny music player. Comes in various formats, some with colour screens to play videos or show your photos.

ISDN
Integrated Services Digital Network. A faster (than standard) Internet connection, requiring a special cable.

ISP
Internet Service Provider. A company which provides you with access to the Internet.

Java and Javascript
A programing language used on some web pages.

JPG or JPEG
Joint Photographic Expert Group. The most commonly used compressed graphic format.

Kilobit (kb)
A thousand bits.

Kilobyte (KB)
A thousand bytes.

LAN
Local Area Network. Computers connected "locally", e.g. within a company or home, so they can communicate and share programs and data.

Laser printer
A printer which uses a laser to create an image on a light-sensitive drum, which then loads toner powder onto paper. Often just black printing Faster and more economical than inkjets.

LED
Light Emitting Diode. Some "laser printers" use this type instead of a laser.

Linux
An operating system (OS), like Windows but free and stable. It requires software written especially for it.

Macro
A small program within another program which, at the touch of a couple of keys performs a series of actions.

Malware
Software which arrives on your computer that is considered to be damaging or have evil intent e.g. viruses, spyware or keyloggers.

Megabit (mb)
A million bits.

Megabyte (MB)
A million bytes. See also Bit, Byte, Kilobyte, Gigabyte, Exabyte.

Megahertz
A measure of how fast your PC processor works. Basically a million vibrations a second. One instruction takes place each vibration.

Mini notebook
A new breed of PC, weighing a couple pounds, with a smaller screen and no CD/DVD drive.

Monitor
The computer screen. Also called a VDU – Visual Display Unit.

Motherboard
The main circuit board of a computer, to which other components are attached.

MP3
A highly compressed form of music, which can be downloaded from the Internet and played on a computer or a portable MP3 player.

MPEG
Motion Picture Expert Group. A method of compressing digital video There are various developments such as MPEG2 and MPEG3.

MSN
Microsoft Network.

Netscape communicator
Netscape's email client program (an alternative to Outlook Express).

Netscape navigator
Netscape's Browser. An alternative to Internet Explorer.

Network
General term for connected computers.

OCR
Optical Character Recognition. Some software can convert scanned text into word-processable documents.

Offline
Not connected to the Internet. Some things, like writing emails, can be done before going online.

Online
Connected to the Internet.

OS
Operation System, such as Windows, Linux or Chrome OS.

Outlook express
The free Microsoft program for handling emails.
Netscape's is called Messenger.

Parallel port
Almost always a 25 pin "female" socket on the back of
a computer which is used for printing but also to attach
things like scanners and other external equipment.

Patch
A software fix for an existing program.

Path
The location of a file or program on a disk, e.g. Word is at
C:\program files\microsoftOffice\office\winword.exe

PCI slot
Peripheral Component Interface (or Interconnect). A type
of connector (slot on the motherboard) – usually white –
which enables you to add components to your PC.

PDA
Personal Digital Assistant. A small, hand-held computer.

Phishing
This is the name give to a scam where you get an email
supposedly from your bank, requesting that you confirm
your password and account number. If you give your
details you can expect your account to be robbed shortly
afterwards! Millions of these emails are sent out and some
gullible people fall for them.

Pixel

Picture element. A small element on a screen or in a photograph. Cameras are sometimes referred to in megapixels. A megapixel is a million pixels. The more pixels the better the quality of the picture and the more memory is used up.

Plug and play

Modern machines and hardware (printers, sound cards, CD players etc) are able to recognize when they are connected, so enabling easy installation or use.

Point size

The height of a printed character. Correspondence is usually around 12 point.

Podcasting

Allowing people to download sounds (news) they can hear on their computer, iPod or MP3 player.

Port

Either a socket on your computer, such as USB, parallel (printer) or serial (communications) OR part of the system which allows communication with your computer (the latter are numbered e.g. Port 110).

Quarantine

When using anti-virus software you may be given the option to do this or delete the offending files. Quarantine allows you to put the item back if your machine starts playing up badly.

Quicktime
A program from Apple which enables you to view moving pictures.

RAM
Random Access Memory. Chips in your PC which work on programs temporarily.

Ransomware
Bad software that appears mysteriously on your PC displaying what appears to be viruses and demanding a fee to get rid of them. One of the biggest scams at the moment.

RAW
A photo file type which is completely unchanged – i.e not compressed, etc. Some photo image software can view them.

Real time
Immediate contact (messages, music, video) rather than via email.

Register
A most important file used in Windows 95 onwards. Contains details of everything within Windows.

Router
A gadget which connects more than one computer to the Internet and sorts out the priorities.

Scanner
A piece of equipment capable of digitally recording a picture or some text for saving on the computer.

Scareware
There are many "free" programs that claim to remove threats from your PC. When you scan your PC they pick up every single "cookie" on the machine and classify it as a threat. They then suggest you buy the full program to clear these "threats". See also Ransomware.

S-video
A higher-quality video connection. It carries brightness and colour information separately.

SCSI
Small Computer System Interface. A fast interface (connection) for attaching peripherals to your computer.

SDRAM
Synchronous Dynamic Random Access Memory. The most common type of memory chip.

Search engine
A program, usually accessed through the Internet, enabling you to search for what you want by entering a few words.

Serial port
A 9 or 25 pin (male) socket on the back of a computer, which can be used to attach a mouse, a modem or a printer. Referred to as a COM (Communication) port Most PCs have two built in.

SMS
Short Message System. Text messages between PC and mobile phone or mobile to mobile.

Site or Website
An area on the Internet that has its own unique web address (URL). It has a Home Page followed by other pages linked to the home page.

Software
Programs of all kinds which make the computer act in a particular way.

SPAM
Unsolicited advertising that usually arrives as emails.

SPIM
Spam which occurs when you are Instant Messaging.

Spyware
Software which is installed on your computer without your knowledge to monitor and report back what you are doing.

Streaming
Receiving sound or pictures continuously over the Internet (rather than downloading first).

Surfing the Web
This means using Hypertext links to jump from one site or page to another.

TAB key
The key on the left of the keyboard which allows you to jump certain fixed distances across the page when using a word processor.

Tablet PC
A powerful Windows PC which has a touch-sensitive flat screen but no attached keyboard. Can be written on with a stylus.

Taskbar/System tray
The bar at the bottom of the screen which shows the items which are pre-installed.

Temporay files
The Internet, some installation programs and even your own programs may use a part of your hard disk to enable them to work. They often end in TMP. They can be deleted later.

Terabyte
1 terabyte (TB) equals 1,000,000,000,000 bytes. Some new hard discs now are able to store that much.

Toolbar
A list of icons often found at the top of a program such as a word processor.

Ttojan
A virus program that is disguised as something else. It invades your PC and can be accessed by a hacker.

URL
Universal (or Unique) Resource Locator or Web address. It always starts with http:// and is usually followed by www and then other parts of the address.

USB port
Universal Serial Bus. A more recent versatile communication port, which can transfer data faster and also enables equipment to be "hot swapped", while the machine is on. The sockets are about 1.25cm (½in)long.

USB2
At 480MB/second is even faster than USB. Looks the same as USB and the slower devices can also be attached to it.

USB3
Much faster than USB2. Unless built in it will be difficult to install, as the card will require a PCIe (PCI-E) slot, not available on machines prior to 2009.

VCD
Video Compact Disc. Stores very compressed videos onto CDs rather than DVDs.

VDU
Visual Display Unit. The screen.

Vector image
A graphic which is made up of instructions to the computer, e.g. to draw a curve or a straight line.

VGA
Video Graphics Array. The older type of colour screen.

Video conferencing
Using the PC as a videophone.

Videophone
Using a microphone, speakers and a webcam to see and hear others over the Internet.

Virtual memory (VM)
When Windows does not find enough RAM, it uses the hard disc rather than failing altogether. This makes the machine seem slower, so more RAM is preferable.

Virus
A malicious program which can harm your computer. It is spread through programs – either from disks or from the Internet. It is the graffiti of the Internet. Viruses may also be called Trojans or Worms.

WAN
Wider Area Network. Computers connected to others over a wide area, so they can communicate and share programs and data.

WAP
Wireless Application Protocol. A system of sending Internet pages to the screen of a mobile phone.

WAP enabled phone – A mobile phone which can receive Internet pages.

Web browser
A program to help you navigate the Internet, e.g. Internet Explorer or Netscape Navigator.

Webcam
A small camera which is attached to a computer.

WI-FI
A wireless interface, using radio to link computers and other devices.

Windows 95
The 1995 version of the Windows system, which replaced version 3.11.

Windows 98
The 1998 version of the Windows system, which replaced Windows 95.

Windows ME
Windows Millennium Edition. A halfway house between Windows 98 and Windows XP.

Windows XP
Microsoft's last operating system, intended to replace all previous Windows formats. There are Home and Professional versions.

Windows 7
Microsoft's most recent operating system, intended to replace all previous Windows formats.

Wizard
A program which helps you through a process such as installing new software or hardware.

WMA
Windows Media Audio. A compressed audio format.

WMV
Windows Media Video. A compressed video format.

Worm
A virus program that spreads by sending itself to people in your email address book.

Zip file
Compressed file that ends in ZIP or CAB. To see their contents they must be viewed using a special program such as Winzip or Enzip.

Zombie
A computer that has been infiltrated by a virus, leaving it open to attacks which "waken it from the dead". These can then be used to send thousands of searches to a particular site, thus bringing it to a standstill. This has happened to Microsoft, Google and Yahoo. Zombies are also used to circulate phishing emails and viruses.

INDEX